Headline Series

BLISHED BY THE FOREIGN POLICY ASSOCIATION NO.223

$1.40

CHINA
HE UNCERTAIN FUTURE

by Harry Harding, Jr.

CHINA:
the Uncertain Future
by Harry Harding, Jr.

CONTENTS

December 1974   Number 223

Cover: Photo, UNICEF; design, Bernard P. Wolff

The Author

Harry Harding, Jr. received his B.A. from Princeton and his Ph.D. in political science from Stanford. During the 1970-71 academic year, he taught politics at Swarthmore College. He then returned to Stanford University to become an assistant professor of political science. His articles have appeared in *Asian Survey* (1971 and 1972), *The Cultural Revolution in China* (1971), *The Annals* (1972), *The Military and Political Power in China in the 1970's* (1972) and *Comparative Defense Policy* (1974). His current research interests include political development and change in China, the management of the Chinese bureaucracy and Sino-American relations.

The Foreign Policy Association

HEADLINE SERIES, No. 223, December 1974, published February, April, June, October and December by the FOREIGN POLICY ASSOCIATION, INC., 345 E. 46th St., New York, N. Y. 10017. President, SAMUEL P. HAYES; HEADLINE SERIES Editor, NORMAN JACOBS; Associate Editor, GWEN CROWE. Subscription rates, $5.00 for 5 issues; $9.00 for 10 issues; $12.00 for 15 issues. Single copies, $1.25. SECOND-CLASS POSTAGE PAID AT NEW YORK, N. Y. Copyright, 1974 by FOREIGN POLICY ASSOCIATION, INC.

Library of Congress Catalog No. 74-22837

History of the Succession

On October 1, 1974, the People's Republic of China celebrated its 25th anniversary. The 25 years since the Communist seizure of power in 1949 have been turbulent ones. China has experienced sudden changes in social and economic policy, serious political conflict and even periods of nationwide disorder. But the possibility of even greater change lies ahead. With Mao Tse-tung now in his 80's, China is confronting with increasing urgency the most significant and complex problem it has faced since 1949: the succession to Mao and the transition to a post-Mao era.

Will China after Mao continue to pursue its present social and economic policies? Or will it adopt new ones? Will China be able to enter the post-Maoist era easily, with strong new leadership and little political conflict? Or will the death of Mao produce a violent struggle for power, widespread social disorder and even economic collapse? Will China continue to improve its relations with the United States, or will it seek a reconciliation with the Soviet Union, at the expense of Sino-American *détente*? Will China maintain a moderate foreign policy, or will it support revolution in the "third world"? No one can answer these vital questions with certainty. But the outcome of China's transition to a post-Maoist era is clearly of crucial importance to Chinese and Americans alike.

The Two 'Lines'

The succession to Mao is not a new problem for China. It first arose as a political issue in the mid-1950's, as Chinese leaders came to realize the desirability of making workable arrangements for the succession well before Mao's death. Since then, they have formulated no less than three plans for the succession, each envisioning different institutions and leaders for a post-Maoist China. But despite their differences, the three arrangements have had one important thing in common: they all encountered considerable opposition within years of their adoption. As a result, the first two plans failed; and the viability of the current succession arrangements remains very much in doubt.

China's first plan for the succession seemed at the time to be a logical one. In essence, it was to construct a collective leadership which could carry on the work of the Communist movement after Mao's death. In order to ensure that power would pass smoothly from Mao to his lieutenants, the Chinese began in 1956 gradually to divide their central leadership into two "lines." While remaining the party chairman, Mao was supposed to retreat to the "second line"—in the rear of the battle, so to speak—where he would devote his time primarily to theoretical and ideological questions. Even when he did take up more immediate, practical problems, the Chinese emphasized that Mao would consult with his colleagues, and not act unilaterally. The party's Politburo and Secretariat, taken collectively, were to become the "first line," responsible for day-to-day policy-making and organizational management. Under this plan, when Mao died, his successors would already be in office, would have had considerable experience in running the country, and thus would be able to provide China with the continuity of leadership necessary to a smooth succession.

Underlying Tensions

From the beginning, however, there was an underlying tension in this division of labor between Mao and his colleagues. Mao claimed during the Cultural Revolution (1966-69) that his withdrawal to the second line was not altogether voluntary. There is good reason to believe that he was right. Some of Mao's colleagues on the Politburo, while enthusiastic about his accomplishments as a revolutionary leader, had come to doubt his suitability to guide China's social and economic modernization. They believed that, the seizure of power completed, it was now time to transfer leadership from "peasant revolutionaries" like Mao to men with greater experience in the administration of large political and economic organizations.

Moreover, Mao began to differ with his colleagues over the best course for Chinese political, social and economic development. In 1955, for instance, there was controversy over the pace of agricultural collectivization. In 1956 there was a debate over policy toward nonparty intellectuals; and in late 1957, a dispute over China's general economic strategy. In each case, Mao was able to use logic and political maneuver to win over the majority of his colleagues. But the results of the Great Leap Forward (1958-59) cost Mao much support. Mao later claimed that, because of the failure of the leap, he was forced to resign the state chairmanship, and was driven even deeper into the second line. As he later put it, he felt that his colleagues were treating him as if he were already dead.

The relatively muted policy disagreements of the 1950's became more severe in the early 1960's. With Mao now almost completely removed from day-to-day decision-making, the power of the first line to set China's course was substantially enhanced. The most important figure in this collective first-line leadership was Liu Shao-ch'i, the first vice-chairman of the party. After Mao's retirement from the post in 1959, Liu became the chairman of the People's Republic, and by 1964 his power rivaled Mao's. Liu was a contemporary of Mao, came from the same province and had been

together with Mao in Yenan in the 1930's and 40's. But his stolid personality, his rather cautious approach to problems and his faith in organization all set him apart from Mao, the flamboyant, romantic and antibureaucratic revolutionary.

It is perhaps not surprising, therefore, that the social, economic and cultural policies adopted by the first line under Liu's leadership ran counter to Mao's vision of China's future. True, these policies were helping stimulate China's economic recovery from the Great Leap Forward and promote a spirit of political reconciliation. But they were also producing economic inequalities in Chinese society, particularly between the cities and the countryside, and were creating, Mao feared, a new bureaucratic elite with attitudes and life styles far different from those of ordinary workers and peasants. Mao charged that these policies were "revisionist," in that they were undermining the values of the Communist revolution. In response to these criticisms, Liu apparently insisted that the policies were still socialist, not revisionist, in character, and that they were necessary and effective measures to help China recover from the economic and political damage caused by the Great Leap Forward.

Was the first line really leading China down a revisionist path? Or was it simply trying to engineer an economic recovery? On these questions, China experts still disagree. But the important and indisputable point is that the creation of two leadership lines was now paralleled by two competing policy lines. Rather than working together, Mao and his apparent successors were now increasingly in conflict.

The Cultural Revolution

Beginning in late 1962 Mao began to intervene more forcefully in the political process in an attempt to reverse some of the first line's policy decisions. During this "socialist education movement," Mao issued a series of statements and instructions on rural policy, education, public health and cultural matters, chiding his colleagues for following the "capitalist" rather than the "proletarian" road. Mao's prestige and authority were still such that the party establishment could not completely ignore these initiatives. But some party leaders did thwart Mao by implementing his directives in a half-hearted manner. By early 1965 Mao had concluded that many of his colleagues, including Liu, would have to be either forced to change their policies or else removed from office. Liu, once seen as Mao's likely successor as party chairman, had now completely lost Mao's confidence.

What began as a debate over policy soon became a struggle for power. Initially, Mao was at a substantial disadvantage, for most of the party apparatus, in both Peking and the provinces, was under the control of his opponents. But Mao had three important resources of his own: the backing of most of the People's Liberation Army (PLA) under Defense Minister Lin Piao; his personal support among many Chinese students and workers, particularly those of lower social and economic standing; and the acquiescence, although not unquestioning support, of Premier Chou En-lai.

In this struggle, Mao took the offensive. In mid-1966, he called on China's high school and university students to form revolutionary organizations known as Red Guards. Later, workers and, to a lesser degree, peasants were also organized into "revolutionary rebel" groups. Acting partly spontaneously, and partly under the guidance of Mao's closest associates in Peking, these organizations began to criticize bureaucrats and party officials throughout the country who had allegedly departed from Maoist policies. Those officials willing to accept mass criticism, admit their "errors" and change their policies could be allowed to "pass the test" and remain in office. Those who resisted the movement, now called the Great Proletarian Cultural Revolution, would be demoted or dismissed.

Purge of Liu

Liu chose to resist. In a serious miscalculation of the strength of Mao's will and the support the chairman could mobilize among

China's youth, Liu tried futilely to bring the Red Guards and the Cultural Revolution under the control of the party apparatus. In Mao's eyes, Liu had been given a final opportunity to redeem himself but had refused to take it. As a result, Liu became one of the Cultural Revolution's first victims. In August 1966 he was stripped of his position as party vice-chairman and Mao's heir apparent. In early 1967 he was effectively dismissed as state chairman, expelled from the Politburo and forced to present lengthy "self-criticisms" to mass rallies held to denounce him. Ultimately, in late 1968, he was expelled from the party altogether and described by a Central Committee communiqué as a "renegade, scab and traitor."

While Mao was able to secure Liu's purge, the Red Guard movement as a whole was unable to achieve the goals that Mao had apparently set for it. Mao believed that in the heat of the struggle, the overwhelming majority of the Chinese people would unite with him in opposition to the revisionist party officials. Actually, what happened was just the opposite: the Red Guard movement fragmented into innumerable competing organizations. Some remained responsive to instructions from the Maoist headquarters in Peking. Others took part in the movement less out of firm political conviction than a spirit of youthful adventure. And still others became even more radical and anarchistic than Mao had intended. They called for the overthrow of all party officials and the replacement of party leadership by a system of grass-roots, participatory democracy. Moreover, the resistance of the party organization, particularly in the provinces, was greater than Mao had anticipated. Instead of responding sincerely and openly to the Red Guards, most officials sought to delay, disrupt or detour the movement, either through outright suppression of Red Guard organizations, or by organizing their own supporters to defend them against attack.

By early 1967, therefore, less than a year after it had begun, it was evident that the Red Guard movement not only had failed to attain Mao's goals, but also had created serious new problems. In

9

most places party officials remained relatively secure in their positions, while the Red Guards fought among themselves. Even where the Red Guards were able to combine enough political force to overthrow local party leaders, they were unable to exercise effectively the power they had seized. Throughout the country, the near-anarchy of the Cultural Revolution threatened to disrupt both industrial and agricultural production.

At this point, Mao turned to his second base of political support—the army. He ordered it to seize power from those provincial party officials who did not support the Cultural Revolution, to establish a temporary military control apparatus to ensure public order and maintain production, and to begin the complicated task of restoring unity to the Red Guards. In this way, the Cultural Revolution, while originally a semispontaneous mass movement, gradually became a political campaign administered by the army.

The Rise of Lin Piao

In calling on the army to "support the left" in the Cultural Revolution, Mao simultaneously promoted China's top military commander, Defense Minister Lin Piao, to be his principal deputy. Lin's spectacular rise to power, from his appointment as defense minister in 1959 to his emergence as Mao's successor in 1966-67, can be traced to three principal factors: his reputation as a man who was committed to Maoist ideology and who could successfully apply it to practical affairs; the growing influence of the army in Chinese politics throughout the 1960's; and Lin's own efforts to increase his control over the military chain-of-command.

After becoming minister of defense in 1959, Lin moved swiftly and decisively to increase the commitment of the People's Liberation Army (PLA) to Maoist ideology. Political education was reemphasized; party organizations within the army, strengthened; the authority of political commissars, increased; personal military ranks and honors, abolished; and guerrilla warfare, enshrined, rhetorically at least, as China's basic strategic principle. It was Lin, in fact, who supervised the compilation of *Quotations from*

Chairman Mao Tse-tung, the famous "little red book" of the Cultural Revolution, as a means of putting Maoist ideology into a form that could readily be used by the ordinary soldier.

At the same time, though, Lin did not ignore his military responsibilities. In programs that sometimes seemed to conflict with his rhetorical advocacy of "people's war," Lin sponsored the rapid development of China's navy, air force and nuclear weapons systems. The PLA's success in the Sino-Indian border war of 1962 and the explosion of China's first atomic bomb in 1964 both testified to the military effectiveness of China's armed forces under Lin's command.

In this way, Lin turned the PLA into an organization that seemed both proficient in its day-to-day responsibilities and imbued with Maoist political values. At a time when Mao saw the state and party as ossified bureaucracies, formulating revisionist policies, the PLA seemed a welcome alternative. And although Mao began to doubt the ideological commitment and personal loyalty of many of his colleagues, he saw Lin—who referred to Mao in 1966 as "the greatest genius in the history of the world"— as a devoted and faithful lieutenant.

Growing Power of Army

Because of these developments, the PLA began to play an increasingly important role in Chinese domestic politics in the 1960's. In 1964 "political departments," staffed by military officers, were established in civilian economic agencies to increase their administrative efficiency and reverse their tendencies toward revisionism. And in 1965 and 1966, when China's other central media seemed to be under the control of Mao's opponents, Mao's associates were able to publish their calls for continued class struggle in the national army newspaper.

The PLA's influence in domestic affairs grew even more dramatically in early 1967, when it was ordered to take responsibility for guiding the Cultural Revolution. When Mao ordered that "revolutionary committees" be created throughout China to take over from the discredited party apparatus, it was the army that supervised their formation. When the composition of the committees was announced, it was frequently military officers who served in the leading positions. By the end of 1968, when the last of the provincial revolutionary committees was selected, PLA officers occupied 66 percent of the chairmanships and 76 percent of the vice-chairmanships, assuming a position of leadership in Chinese society unknown since the early 1950's.

Growing Power of Lin

In itself, the growing power of the army clearly helped increase Lin's political influence in Peking. But behind the scenes Lin was simultaneously attempting to improve his own position within the PLA. Although holding the formal position of minister of defense, Lin had had to cope with the interservice and interpersonal rivalries characteristic of most large military forces. Now, the Cultural Revolution helped Lin increase his influence within the army. One of the earliest victims of the Cultural Revolution was Lin's chief rival in the army, Chief of Staff Lo Jui-ch'ing, who was purged in late 1965. Then, in 1967, Lin secured the dismissal or demotion of other important central, regional and provincial military commanders, replacing many of them with close personal associates. By the end of the year, while his control of the PLA was not at all absolute, Lin had scored striking successes in an effort to turn the army into what might be called a personal political machine.

For all these reasons, then, Lin seemed in 1969 to be the logical choice as Mao's successor. He appeared devoted to Maoist values, seemed loyal to Mao personally, had a highly creditable record as defense minister and controlled an organization which was essential to the maintenance of political order and economic production. Not surprisingly, therefore, the Ninth Party Congress, convened in April 1969 to consolidate the accomplishments of the Cultural Revolution, officially designated Lin as Mao Tse-tung's "closest comrade-in-arms and successor."

And yet, as he left the Congress, Lin must have wondered how secure his position was. The Cultural Revolution had deeply fragmented Chinese politics, and the new leadership elected at the Ninth Congress was marked by serious disunity. Although Lin was able to secure the election of several of his closest associates to the Politburo, they were joined by Cultural Revolution radicals, party bureaucrats who had survived the Cultural Revolution, and some important central and regional military commanders who were not closely linked to Lin. Moreover, the Chinese have recently revealed, Lin suffered the humiliation of having the first draft of his speech to the Congress rejected by Mao. As Chou En-lai later explained, "Although Lin Piao had become the successor at the Ninth Congress, his mind was not at ease. He knew that he could not really become the successor."

Maneuvers of Lin

Lin was not satisfied with this situation. He wanted to ensure that he would be Mao's successor in fact as well as in name, and that potential rivals would not be able to unseat him before Mao's death. After the Ninth Congress, therefore, he sought every opportunity to bolster his position in the Chinese political arena.

The reconstruction of the party after the Ninth Congress provided Lin with one such chance. New party committees were being formed throughout the country to replace those denounced and discredited during the Cultural Revolution, with the PLA again supervising the selection of committee members. According to later Chinese charges, Lin tried to replace as many veteran party officials as possible during this party reorganization, claiming that they had "failed the test" of the Cultural Revolution. In their place, he sought to appoint military officers, preferably men with whom he had personal or institutional ties. If these charges are true, Lin was attempting to form a personal clique within the party, similar to the one he had constructed in the PLA only a few years before.

Lin also tried to win appointment to the state chairmanship, the post formerly occupied by Liu Shao-ch'i. This would have given

Lin at least nominal authority over the state bureaucracy, usually considered the preserve of Premier Chou En-lai; it would also have formally made him commander-in-chief of the Chinese armed forces. Taken together with his position as sole party vice-chairman, the state chairmanship would have placed Lin second only to Mao in the party, state and military hierarchies.

A third strategy Lin may have employed was to ally with at least one of the leading radicals of the Cultural Revolution: Ch'en Po-ta, an important party theorist, former secretary to Mao, member of the Standing Committee of the Politburo and head of the Cultural Revolution Group, the coordinating body of the Red Guard movement. Together with Ch'en, Lin apparently took a rather radical position on a wide range of issues confronting China in 1970 and 1971. He favored a harsh policy toward former party officials removed from office during the Cultural Revolution. He opposed the emerging *rapprochement* with the United States. Moreover, some analysts believe that Lin may have challenged China's prevailing economic policies by advocating greater investment in heavy industry (particularly electronics), restrictions on the size of private peasant plots, and a program to redistribute resources from wealthier to poorer agricultural production teams. By taking this radical line, Lin may have hoped to win the support of the other radicals on the Politburo and thus gain a working majority. Furthermore, he may have believed that adopting radical positions would underline his commitment to Mao, and thus ensure the chairman's continued personal support. Both these considerations would help isolate Chou, whom Lin must have seen as his foremost potential rival.

Lin's Fall from Power

Unfortunately for Lin, this set of strategies served more to undermine his position than to strengthen it. His sponsorship of radical economic and foreign policies, predictably, encountered the opposition of more moderate leaders. The decisive factor in Lin's fall, though, was that he miscalculated Mao's thinking on several important issues. From the available evidence, Mao was an enthusiastic supporter—perhaps even the initiator—of "ping-pong" diplomacy with the United States. Lin's criticism of the opening to Washington was, indirectly, a criticism of Mao. Too, Mao apparently was not convinced of the wisdom of altering China's post-Cultural Revolutionary economic policies. And finally, Mao concluded that Lin's demands for the state chairmanship and for the perpetuation of military participation in civilian decision-making reflected unseeming ambition—and even a challenge to Mao's ultimate authority.

The first direct confrontation between Mao and Lin occurred at a Central Committee meeting in September 1970, when the two men clashed over the question of the state chairmanship. In characteristic fashion, Mao began to undermine Lin's position, while giving his "comrade-in-arms" at least a nominal chance to redeem himself. Mao threw his weight against Lin's position on several important policy questions, agreed to the purge of Lin's radical ally Ch'en Po-ta and one of Lin's closest military supporters, and began criticizing the "arrogance and complacency" of senior military commanders.

What happened next may never be satisfactorily known. The Chinese charge that Lin, realizing that his position was growing weaker, launched a plot to stage an armed *coup d'état* against Mao, Chou and the rest of the party leadership in Peking. (The Chinese also claim that Lin sought Soviet support for his intrigues.) As an opening maneuver, the Chinese say, Lin dispatched agents to assassinate the chairman, but they were foiled on three separate occasions. His plan now revealed, Lin made a last minute attempt to flee to the Soviet Union, but died when his jet transport crashed in Outer Mongolia in September 1971.

Some Western observers remain unconvinced of the accuracy of this account of Lin's fall from power. They point out that it might simply be an attempt to exaggerate Lin's crimes—and therefore explain to skeptical local cadres why Lin, formerly described as Mao's "best pupil," "closest comrade-in-arms," and "worthy successor," had to be removed from office. A less dramatic, but perhaps more plausible explanation of Lin's purge might be that Lin sought a political rather than a military showdown with Mao after their first confrontation in September 1970. When the final crisis came in August and September 1971, however, it was Mao and not Lin who was able to win the majority of China's provincial and central party leaders. Realizing that he had lost the struggle, and fearing what might happen if he remained in China, Lin may then have made his unsuccessful bid to escape to the Soviet Union.

Chou En-lai as Succession Manager

The fall of Lin Piao, and the simultaneous collapse of China's second attempt to arrange the succession to Mao, brought Premier Chou En-lai to the center of the Chinese political stage. But Chou did not assume the position of heir apparent to Mao, as both Liu and Lin had done. For one thing, at age 76, Chou was only four years the chairman's junior, and thus could not be expected to live much longer than Mao himself. For another, Chou and Mao apparently agreed to form a new collective leadership, rather than to try once again to appoint a single successor. "With such a big country and the problems facing us," Chou said in an interview in 1972, "how can you have only one successor?" Thus, rather than a successor, Chou became more of a "succession manager," attempting to rebuild the political institutions shattered during the Cultural Revolution and to form a viable collective leadership which can survive the death of Mao.

By mid-1973, Chou had made substantial progress along these lines. The Tenth Party Congress, convened in August, legitimated the purge of Lin Piao and confirmed the composition of a new Politburo, assembled under Chou's guidance. China seemed well on the road toward greater political and institutional stability. Within a year, however, Chou's management of the succession suffered two serious blows. The first was a strong challenge from more radical leaders; they charged that the moderate foreign and domestic policies Chou had sponsored since 1971 had betrayed the purposes and accomplishments of the Cultural Revolution. The second was Chou's own deteriorating health, which forced his hospitalization in mid-1974. Both these problems will be discussed in more detail later. But their main effect was to bring the future of this, China's third plan for the succession, into considerable doubt.

Implications for the Future

These recent developments have only served to deepen the conflict and controversy that have surrounded the question of the succession in China since the mid-1950's. The events of the past 20 years seem to bear several related lessons for Chinese political leaders. First, no succession arrangement, no matter how closely it seems to be associated with Mao, should be regarded as stable or permanent. As the fates of Liu and Lin show, Mao himself may turn against the very men he once named as his successors.

Second, because of this, it is entirely feasible for those who object to existing succession arrangements to challenge them, particularly if they believe they can cause Mao to lose confidence in his heir apparent. Conversely, no man named as Mao's successor can ever feel secure, but must constantly try to bolster his political position against attack by his rivals.

Third, because of its importance as an issue, succession has been the occasion for intrigue and even violence in Chinese politics. Mao's willingness to go outside the party and mobilize the masses in his assault on Liu, and Lin's alleged plan to assassinate Mao, both indicate that Chinese leaders may violate previously established rules of the game in order to influence the succession.

In short, the history of the succession suggests that Chinese leaders may have lost much of their earlier ability to handle conflict and dissent through compromise and accommodation. The historical legacy of suspicion, intrigue, instability and violence that surround the succession has done much to reduce the chances that China can make the transition to a post-Maoist society in a smooth and peaceful manner.

The Issue of Modernization

One important trend in Chinese politics between 1949 and 1966 was increasing disagreement among Chinese leaders over a wide range of social and economic issues. Obviously, even in the early years of the People's Republic, there was never complete unanimity over social or economic policy. But Chinese leaders in the early 1950's did manage to exhibit a surprising degree of consensus on the goals they wished to attain and the means they would use to pursue them. By 1957, however, this consensus had begun to break apart, and by the middle 1960's deep cleavages had emerged within the Chinese elite on a large number of important policy issues. This growing conflict was a major factor leading to the Cultural Revolution.

In similar fashion, these issues will have an important impact on the succession process. Do the policy differences still exist, or did the Cultural Revolution resolve them? If they persist, they may lead to serious conflict at the time of Mao's death, as contenders in the succession struggle to implement their own vision of China's future. If, on the other hand, they can be resolved or compromised, the chances for a smooth succession will be enhanced.

What are the issues at stake? They touch virtually every aspect of Chinese social and economic life, from industrial management to public health, from employment policy to primary education, from agricultural mechanization to industrial wages. They are too numerous to describe in detail here. But we can identify an overarching theme that ties them together: What is the proper course for China's social and economic modernization?

If asked to identify his party's basic goal, a Chinese leader might well reply that it was to continue his country's socialist construction, and ultimately build a Communist society. If pressed further, he probably would indicate that this rather abstract aim had two more specific components. First, it would entail the transformation of China—still a relatively poor, agricultural society—into a modern industrial state, capable of taking its place as a strong, independent member of the international community. A second component would be to reduce, and ultimately eliminate, all social and economic inequalities in China: between fertile and nonfertile areas, manager and worker, officer and soldier, old and young, city and countryside, party official and ordinary citizen. To put it another way, China's stated aim is to ensure that both the costs and benefits of modernization are spread fairly among all China's geographic regions and occupational groups.

While, in theory, all Chinese leaders seem to accept these two goals, they have had severe disputes about how to implement them. One problem is that economic development and socioeconomic equality often conflict with each other. Sometimes, the toleration—or even the deliberate promotion—of inequality has seemed a necessary price to pay for rapid industrialization and economic growth. Faced with this dilemma, Chinese leaders have been forced to set priorities between development and equality. And the evidence indicates that some have opted for equality, others for development and still others for a balance between the two.

Agriculture

By any standard, agriculture is crucial to China's economic future. Even with a relatively effective birth control program, China's population, estimated by the U.S. government today at around 835 million people, is expected to reach one billion by 1980 and 1.3 billion by 1990. As a result, China will have to increase its agricultural production by a little more than 2 percent per year simply to keep up with its rising population.

But China is not satisfied simply with keeping up. Like all developing countries, China wants to raise living standards through industrialization. And agriculture is essential to industrial growth. The agricultural sector provides raw materials for industry; export products with which to import advanced technology; and food, clothing and consumer goods for a growing urban labor force. The crucial connection between industry and agriculture can be seen clearly by looking at China's economic record since 1949. Whenever agricultural production has fallen or leveled off—as in 1953, 1956 and 1959—industrial production has also declined within one or two years. But when agricultural production has increased, Chinese industry has enjoyed higher, sustained rates of growth.

Clearly, then, industrial development depends on agriculture. But to what extent does agricultural development, in turn, depend on the industrial sector? This is a question on which Chinese leaders have frequently been divided. If industry must provide machinery, pesticides, fertilizers and other products for the countryside, its own development will be restricted. Conversely, if agriculture can grow independently, without relying on the industrial sector, then industrial development will be all the more rapid. The temptation for some Chinese planners, therefore, has been to try to minimize the flow of machinery and supplies from industry into agriculture.

Two Plans

In the 1950's, two such plans were attempted. Under the First

Plowing a rice paddy on Chinese commune

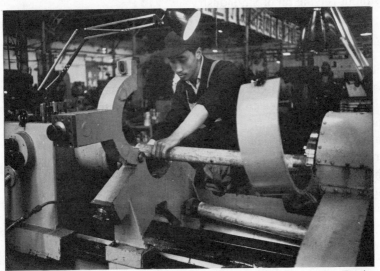

Anshan Iron and Steel Factory

Five-Year Plan (1953-57), modeled after the Soviet experience, state investment in agriculture was kept to a minimum. Instead, Chinese planners sought to increase agricultural productivity by combining the small family farms created by land reform into larger, more efficient collective farms. Then, during the Great Leap Forward (1958-59), the countryside was reorganized once again, this time into even larger communes, each consisting of an average of 5,000 households. In each case, the goal was to achieve economies of scale by pooling labor power, land, tools and animals into larger and larger units of production.

Beyond this, the Great Leap Forward also attempted to generate new investment in agriculture through the massive mobilization of rural manpower. Armies of peasants were deployed in the construction of flood control and irrigation projects. Small "backyard" steel furnaces and factories were opened in the communes so that the peasants could produce their own tools and implements without relying on urban industry.

Unfortunately, both the First Five-Year Plan and the Great Leap Forward had serious shortcomings as blueprints for Chinese agricultural development. Under the First Five-Year Plan, agricultural production fell far behind the needs of the rapidly expanding industrial sector. Consequently, in 1956-57, Chinese planners were forced to reduce industrial investment, and thus industrial growth. During the Great Leap Forward, after striking initial gains, the agricultural economy virtually collapsed, with grain production falling 20 percent between 1958 and 1960. In part, this was due to poor weather, but responsibility must also be laid to the irrationalities in the design and implementation of the leap: the communes proved too large to be operated efficiently; the water conservancy projects, built in haste, were poorly constructed; the metal produced by the backyard steel furnaces was too brittle to be used. And because of the sharp decline in agricultural output, Chinese industry experienced a serious depression in 1959-61 from which it did not fully recover until 1966.

Priority to Agriculture

By the early 1960's, therefore, most Chinese leaders had learned an important lesson: while industry might register spectacular short-term gains at the expense of agriculture, it could not enjoy sustained growth unless it also contributed to agricultural development. As a result, less emphasis was placed on the reorganization of agriculture after 1959. In fact, the communes were reduced in size, and operational authority delegated to small production teams, each consisting of about 20 to 40 households. Instead of relying on economies of scale, the Chinese planners increased the manufacture of tractors, water pumps, electric motors, chemical fertilizers, pesticides and other products required in the rural areas. The idea was that agricultural development should receive the highest priority in economic planning and that industry should aid agriculture by shifting production toward rural needs.

This principle was implemented even more vigorously during the Cultural Revolution—and had implications for virtually every sector of Chinese society. State trading companies were ordered to reduce the prices of products sold to the countryside and raise the prices paid for agricultural products. The army dispatched soldiers to rural areas to help in the busy planting and harvesting seasons. Educational and scientific institutions changed their curricula and research programs to emphasize subjects related to agricultural development. The bureaucracy ordered officials at all levels to pay special attention to rural problems and to gain personal experience by working in the villages under their jurisdiction. And factories were encouraged to send technicians and unneeded equipment to help promote the development of small-scale industry in the rural areas.

The result has been slow but steady growth in agricultural output. Grain production, estimated at around 200 million metric tons before the Cultural Revolution, is approximately 250 million tons today, increasing at an average rate of 3 to 4 percent per year. But Chinese agriculture is still subject to the vagaries of nature. In years when China has suffered from poor weather, insect plagues or plant disease, as in 1972, agricultural production has fallen off as much as 4 percent. Most Chinese planners argue that this demonstrates the need for continuing with present policies of investment in agriculture. If China can produce more fertilizers and pesticides, improved seed strains, better water conservancy facilities and more agricultural machinery, then it will be better able to control nature and ride out natural disasters.

Nevertheless, agricultural policy remains controversial in China. Industrial planners consistently complain that they are being forced to subsidize agriculture, and that this is holding back industrial growth. Some military leaders linked with Lin Piao apparently called for less investment in agriculture and more rapid development of weapons-related industries. Even educators and scientists have said that basic scientific research and training is being sacrificed for the sake of the diffusion of simple agricultural technology. And some radicals have criticized China's rural policy as emphasizing "machines" over "men," claiming that it ignores the possibility of even more rapid growth through mass mobilization. At present though, these critics of current agricultural policy are in the minority, largely because present policies have produced substantial gains over the past several years, and because the critics have been unable to formulate persuasive alternatives. But disagreement persists, and conflict could recur as economic conditions change.

Industry

A second important issue in China concerns the scale and location of industrial investment. It is here that the question of equity versus efficiency in industrial development is particularly evident.

When the Chinese Communists took power in 1949, China's small industrial plant was concentrated in a few regions, principally in Manchuria and along the eastern seaboard. Since then, the Chinese have begun to create new industrial centers in the vast interior of the country, so as to spread the benefits of industrialization more widely across the land. But setting up new industries in previously backward areas—areas lacking the transportation and other economic infrastructure industrial development requires—can be expensive. One issue, then, has been how quickly, and at how great a price, should China foster regional economic equality?

A related problem concerns the scale of industrial investment. Should China emphasize large-scale, capital-intensive industries, located near major urban centers and controlled directly from Peking? Or should it place higher priority on small-scale factories, using simple machinery, located in rural areas and managed by local authorities? The first alternative, implemented during the First Five-Year Plan and, in modified form, during the early 1960's, may lead to more rapid growth, but it widens the gap between city and countryside. The second alternative, practiced during the Great Leap Forward, brings industrialization to rural areas, but, as the backyard steel furnaces showed, may be less efficient economically.

During the Cultural Revolution, in an attempt to reduce the inequalities between city and countryside and between industrialized and nonindustrialized regions, Chinese leaders decided to decentralize and disperse the economy as far as was economically feasible. In practice, this meant that China's industrial system was divided into two tiers. The first tier—China's 29 provinces—became the focus for heavy industry. Each province, it was proposed, should become a "small but complete" industrial system, self-reliant in steel, energy and heavy machinery. Many industries that before the Cultural Revolution were directly controlled from Peking were transferred to provincial management, with central ministries retaining control of industries directly related to national defense.

The second tier of the economy consisted of China's 2,000 counties and 75,000 communes. Most of these have now developed light industries to process and sell agricultural commodities such as seed oil and textiles. The profits from these light industries have then been used to construct the so-called "five small industries": producing electricity, cement, iron and steel, fertilizer and agricultural machinery for local needs. Like the provinces, the counties and communes have been urged to meet their own needs for energy, machinery and construction materials to the greatest extent possible.

Debate Over Industrialization

These two concepts, decentralization and self-reliance, have been controversial—even more controversial than agricultural policy. Their proponents have argued that decentralization would facilitate coordination of local economic activity and local participation in economic decision-making. A "cellular" economy, composed of self-reliant provinces, counties and communes would spread the benefits of industrialization more widely throughout the country, ease the burden on China's inadequate transportation network and increase China's ability to survive a foreign invasion. Finally, they have noted that China has enjoyed a substantial rate of industrial growth since the Cultural Revolution—perhaps 10 percent per year. This shows, they have concluded, that the political, social and military benefits of the policy are not outweighed by substantial economic costs.

Other planners, however, have pointed to the disadvantages of a cellular, decentralized economy. They have argued that the attempt to create a small but complete industrial system in every province—including the more backward ones—is economically impractical. Why, they have asked, should all 29 provinces build automobile assembly plants when fewer would do? They have also claimed that the five small industries in rural areas tend to be too small to be efficient. It is better, they have suggested, to construct a smaller number of bigger, more efficient factories than to spread China's limited resources too thin. And those larger factories should be constructed wherever the investment will bring the highest return, even if that means placing them in the regions that are already more highly industrialized.

By 1973 these critics had gathered enough support to win at least minor adjustments in China's industrial policy. There was a growing tendency to recentralize some branches of heavy industry, and the slogan of small but complete provincial industrial systems was explicitly revoked. In the rural economy, too, Chinese planners began to take a closer look at the five small industries, closing or consolidating some of those located in less-fertile communes. In essence, these changes meant that the richest provinces, counties and communes would tend to become even richer. They meant, in other words, that geographical equality was being sacrificed, to a degree at least, in favor of economic efficiency.

City and Countryside

A third crucial problem in Chinese development has been the social, as well as economic, gap between city and countryside. This problem, which China shares with other parts of the third world, can be traced to the tendency to concentrate key social services—hospitals, schools and universities—in urban areas. While this has an economic logic, it also means that urban residents have easier access to social services than do commune dwellers. It is not surprising, therefore, that literacy rates and school attendance rates are higher and death rates lower in China's cities than in the rural areas.

Unlike many third world countries, however, China has taken dramatic steps to remedy this situation, particularly in the areas of education and public health. While similar reforms were undertaken during the Great Leap Forward, the measures adopted during the Cultural Revolution seem more carefully planned, more effective and thus more likely to be lasting.

In public health, one important reform was the extension of medical facilities to more remote rural areas, many of which had no access to medical care before the Cultural Revolution. The Chinese press reports that nearly all communes now have small-scale medical clinics, many of which are staffed by doctors dispatched from urban hospitals. In addition, some 70 percent of the production brigades (each of which consists on the average of 170 households) are said to have smaller "health stations." These are manned by China's famous "barefoot doctors"—paramedical

27

personnel who have received short-term education in both traditional Chinese and modern Western medicine. The barefoot doctors, over one million of whom were educated during the Cultural Revolution, are trained to promote birth control, practice preventive medicine, treat simple ailments on the spot and send patients with more serious diseases to commune clinics or urban hospitals.

Similar reforms have been implemented in primary and secondary education. Before the Cultural Revolution, many rural youth had little opportunity to attend class, largely because the school buildings were located far from their homes. Now, primary education (which in China has been shortened to five years) has been extended to the production brigade, with a goal of enrolling more than 90 percent of school-age rural youth. Most communes have established junior middle schools, with a two-year curriculum, providing continued education to some 80 percent of the primary school graduates. While still short of the mark, these reforms have moved China closer to its aim of universal seven-year education.

Few would deny that the extension of educational and medical facilities into the Chinese countryside is an admirable goal. But it has encountered budgetary problems. The state budget is not large enough to finance all of the new schools and clinics established during the Cultural Revolution, but without government support, the rural areas are unable to afford adequate facilities. The Chinese admit, for example, that only one-third of the commune clinics presently receive central subsidies and that the others cannot afford to purchase satisfactory medical equipment. With China's resources spread thin, some medical and educational professionals have warned that attempts to provide universality may lead to unacceptable reductions in quality. Others respond that even minimal education and medical care are better than none at all.

As in so many other issues, the outcome of this debate depends on the health of the overall economy. Local schools and clinics were established during the Great Leap Forward, but many were forced to close during the 1959-61 depression. If the Chinese economy should suffer another downturn, Chinese leaders will be faced with a difficult choice: What price are they willing to pay to reduce the urban-rural gap?

Incentives

Finally, Chinese leaders have consistently confronted the problem of material reward as an incentive for work. To what extent, they asked themselves, are material incentives necessary to stimulate Chinese workers and peasants to work hard and produce more? Or can productivity be increased simply through an effective program of ideological exhortation and patriotic appeals?

No Chinese would advocate a return to the system of income distribution which prevailed before 1949, in which there were enormous and unjust differences between the income of a few landlords and wealthy businessmen on the one hand, and the vast majority of peasants and urban laborers on the other. But some Chinese leaders—the majority, in fact—do appear to believe that, in a socialist society, a reasonable system of material incentives is necessary to increase productivity.

Other, more radical Chinese leaders have disagreed, however. Citing the Marxist principle that, under communism, distribution of income should be "to each according to his needs," they have proposed the rapid elimination of material incentives. Continued reliance on material reward, these radicals have argued, creates inequality, fosters a spirit of selfishness and competitiveness rather than sacrifice and cooperation, and thus is incompatible with progress toward a Communist society.

The Great Leap Forward was one attempt to implement these highly egalitarian ideals, particularly in rural areas. Private plots, on which peasants could grow food for their own tables and for sale at state-run markets, were abolished on the grounds that they represented the vestiges of "peasant capitalism." A "free supply" system of income distribution was instituted, under which Chinese peasants were promised all the food they needed, without regard to the amount of work they performed. At the same time, an intensive propaganda campaign was launched, promising the peasants that, if they worked their hardest, China could "catch up with Britain in 15 years."

This reliance on ideological incentives, and the egalitarian system of wage payments that accompanied it, disappeared during the depression of the early 1960's. The earlier system of material incentives, private plots and free markets was restored. During the Cultural Revolution, many Red Guards once again denounced material rewards as incompatible with China's Communist ideology and Mao's egalitarian ideals. Interestingly, however, the Cultural Revolution saw only limited and fleeting attempts to alter the system of material incentives. Apparently, Chinese leaders had concluded that the egalitarian experiment conducted during the Great Leap Forward did not warrant repeating.

What forms do material incentives take in the Chinese economic system today? In the rural areas, Chinese peasants still own small private plots of land, usually amounting to 5 or 6 percent of the land area of each commune, on which they grow vegetables and fruit and raise pigs and chickens. What they do not directly consume, the peasants can sell at rural markets. Thus, the more they produce, the more they can sell—and the more income they can receive.

Collective grain production is also stimulated by a system of material rewards. Peasants are paid according to the quantity and quality of the work they perform, so that those who work harder earn more. And to motivate production teams to exceed their grain production quota, the state agrees to buy any surplus production for 30 percent more than the normal price.

In industry, too, a commitment to the principle of material incentives is clearly evident. Recent visitors to China report that factories still have a graded wage-scale, with the highest-paid administrators receiving about 10 times more than the apprentices and part-time employees at the bottom of the scale. In addition, the Chinese offer substantial material bonuses to workers and workshops that consistently exceed their production targets.

In short, while disparities in income have been reduced since

1949, China is not—nor does it claim to be—a completely egalitarian society. Furthermore, some experts predict that differences among individual incomes will even increase as Chinese planners come to appreciate the value of graded wage systems as a means of economic control. If so, the question of incentives may once again become a central issue in Chinese politics.

Implications for the Succession

Although there are still disagreements over social and economic policy in China, a sizable consensus on China's strategy of modernization seems to have emerged since the Cultural Revolution. True, the Lin Piao affair seems to have demonstrated that this consensus is by no means unanimous. The evidence suggests that Lin was able to assemble a small coalition of radicals, military leaders and industrial planners, all of whom apparently opposed China's current policy of emphasizing the modernization of agriculture over the expansion of industry. But Lin's failure to attract broader support indicates that critics of China's present economic policies are a decided minority.

This consensus on development policy has emerged for three basic reasons. First, Chinese leaders have increasingly realized that there are no viable alternatives to the continued use of material incentives or to the modernization of agriculture through substantial state investment. The two alternatives proposed in the past—the single-minded industrialization of the First Five-Year Plan and the equally single-minded egalitarianism of the Great Leap Forward—both failed abjectly. The critics of present policies may complain, but they have not yet been able to formulate any attractive alternatives.

Second, present policies on the allocation of industrial investment and the distribution of social services represent a seemingly effective compromise between those who seek economic efficiency and those who promote equality. In industry, for example, the local factories established during the Cultural Revolution seem more viable than those built during the Great Leap Forward. In education and public health, the policy of extending services deeper into the countryside in a relatively inexpensive manner, while not beyond criticism, has received widespread support.

Finally, nothing succeeds like success—and China's present economic policies appear to be successful. China's total industrial and agricultural output is estimated to have increased about 8 percent per year since the Cultural Revolution. While this is not a spectacular rate of growth (it is not, for example, as high as the rates achieved by South Korea or Taiwan), it is enough to keep per capita production rising by about 6 percent per year.

Despite these considerations, two potential problems lie ahead. The first is that Chinese leaders will increasingly have to consider the question of allocation of investment within different sectors of industry, particularly among weapons production, the manufacture of consumer goods and the production of capital equipment. The "guns versus butter versus machines" problem could create serious disagreements over economic development strategy.

Even more important, if China's present policies prove unable to continue to increase production at respectable rates, the present consensus behind them could easily collapse. A series of poor harvests, for example, with a concomitant reduction in the rate of industrial growth, would almost certainly lead to demands that greater inequality be tolerated for the sake of recovery. Radicals would equally certainly resist such proposals, arguing that a campaign of mass mobilization could restore higher rates of growth without compromising present levels of socioeconomic equality. In other words, poor economic performance could well force China to face once again the continuing dilemma of economic efficiency and growth versus social and economic equality.

Continuing the Revolution

Discussions of the succession in China tend to focus rather narrowly on the selection of a single successor to Mao Tse-tung, or the formation of a collective, post-Maoist leadership. Actually, the problem is broader than this. The succession involves not simply one man, or even a small group of men, but rather an entire generation: the veteran Communist cadres, now in their 60's, 70's or even 80's, who founded the party, guided it successfully through the revolution and then continued to lead it after the formation of the People's Republic. In a society that greatly values age and experience, this generation has occupied the highest positions in the Chinese political system—not simply in Peking but also in the provinces and localities. Despite its revolutionary values and its commitment to sweeping change, China remains very much a gerontocracy.

Now, however, this senior generation is beginning to pass from the Chinese political scene, and younger men are starting to come to power. To Mao Tse-tung, the death of the "Long March generation" has posed some worrisome questions: Will the younger generations be less committed than their predecessors to the party's revolutionary goals? Will the party retain its original vision of a China that is both industrialized and egalitarian? Or will it give up its utopian goals, gradually lose its revolutionary dynamism and tolerate continued inequality in Chinese society? In short, will it continue the revolution or become revisionist?

Mao's concern with revisionism has occupied a central place in his thinking and writing since the middle 1950's, and the Chinese claim that it represents his most original contribution to the Marxist-Leninist tradition. In essence, Mao has traced the origins of revisionism to two important trends: the gradual bureaucratization of the party and the failure of education, particularly higher education, to imbue China's youth with revolutionary values. Unless these trends can be reversed, Mao has argued, China will eventually see the erosion of revolutionary commitment and increasing tolerance of the *status quo*. Much of the Cultural Revolution, therefore, represented Mao's attempts to reform both bureaucracy and university in order to prevent the emergence of revisionism in China.

Bureaucratization

One of the most controversial questions in the study of modern China concerns the reasons for the Communists' success in their long and arduous struggle against the warlords, the Japanese and Chiang Kai-shek's Nationalist government. How did the Chinese Communist party, numbering a mere handful of men when it was founded in 1921, come into power 28 years later to rule more than 500 million Chinese? Increasingly, scholars are focusing on the ability of the Communists to learn the grievances of the Chinese villages, educate the peasants in the goals and programs of the Communist movement and then translate the peasants' grievances into effective support for the party. The Communist victory in 1949, in other words, was largely one of political organization and was based on the organizational techniques that the Chinese Communists had formulated and tested in their long march to power.

Two of these techniques were particularly important in the

Communists' success. One was a preference for periodic *ad hoc* campaigns as a means of implementing party policy. During these intense campaigns, the party would use ideological, patriotic and economic appeals to mobilize the peasants to carry out its social and economic programs. A second technique, perfected in the early years, relied on continued ideological education of party and government officials, or cadres. Through propaganda, small group discussions and "self-criticism" sessions, cadres were urged to increase their efficiency and discipline, and to make sure that their decisions were compatible with party policy.

After 1949, however, these two techniques slowly began to lose some of their appeal. With the completion of land reform and agricultural collectivization in the 1950's, some Chinese leaders came to believe that most of the problems for which mass campaigns might be appropriate had already been solved. And with the inauguration of nationwide economic planning in 1954, there was a need for greater continuity, sophistication and efficiency in economic management. As a result, most party leaders concluded that China would have to place greater emphasis on bureaucratic procedures and rely less on mass campaigns than it did before 1949. The temporary revival of the campaign style during the unsuccessful Great Leap Forward only strengthened the view of many that bureaucratic organizations provided a more predictable and effective method of implementing economic policy.

In addition, the party found that ideology, while still useful in setting ultimate goals, did not provide the solutions to the innumerable practical problems of day-to-day policy-making and administration. Gradually, policy-making became more pragmatic, Chinese leaders concerning themselves more with results than with the doctrinal justifications for their decisions. Simultaneously, ideological education within the bureaucracy became more ritualized and less intense, with cadres learning how to pass through rectification campaigns with the least effort.

Neither of these trends should be exaggerated. Compared to many other countries, China remained committed to a mobilizational and ideological style of politics. Compared to its own revolutionary past, however, the Chinese Communist movement had become substantially bureaucratized and pragmatic.

Organizational Problems

By the early 1960's, the Chinese bureaucracies had several achievements to their credit. They had established an impressive degree of control over China's vast territory and large population. They had implemented major social and economic reforms in the 1950's and had engineered China's recovery from the Great Leap Forward. But despite these accomplishments, Mao remained skeptical about so marked a departure from the party's organizational heritage. As Mao saw it, many bureaucratic officials, ensconced in comfortable offices, had become divorced from the people they were supposed to serve. Intent upon their day-to-day administrative problems, they had little concern with the ultimate goals of the revolution. Caught in bureacratic routine, they had become lazy and inefficient. Seeking the privileges and perquisites of rank, they looked for ways of climbing higher up the bureaucratic ladder.

Most important of all, the increasing bureaucratization of the party and the state organizations occurred at the same time that China began, in Mao's eyes at least, to adopt revisionist policies. Mao concluded that the growth of the bureaucracy was one of the principal sources of revisionism in China.

One goal of the Cultural Revolution, therefore, was to reform China's political organizations, to make them more responsive to public demands, more committed to revolutionary values and more efficient in their implementation of party policy. Only sweeping organizational reform, Mao felt, could ensure that China would continue to follow the proletarian rather than the revisionist road.

Organizational Revolution

The Cultural Revolution saw experimentation with two quite different types of organizational change. At the height of the Red

Guard movement in early 1967, the goal seemed to be to overthrow all officials, destroy the entire bureaucratic apparatus and replace it with a system of participatory democracy. At the same time, the country was told that "politics" should "take command of everything." This meant that all Chinese should consider the ideological implications of all their actions. No decision, no matter how trivial, was said to be completely devoid of ideological considerations. And no order, no matter how seemingly routine, was to be obeyed unless the recipient was convinced that it corresponded with Maoist doctrine.

The proponents of this organizational revolution—who probably did not include Mao—were undoubtedly sincere, but were also naïve. Despite the claims of some Red Guards that bureaucrats were unnecessary, the collapse of public administration in early 1967 convinced most Chinese that their country still needed formal bureaucratic organization. And the notion that "politics should take command" led to serious confusion and conflict, as people throughout the country puzzled over the implications of Mao's vague ideological pronouncements and then bitterly attacked those whose interpretations differed from their own.

Three Reforms

Because of these problems, this period of organizational revolution was relatively brief. It was replaced by a period of milder reform, in which the goal was to prune back the undesirable aspects of bureaucracy, rather than pull the entire organization up by the roots. Of the many reforms adopted during 1967-69, three are particularly important.

The first was a restructuring of the entire state and party organizational network. The size of the bureaucracy, particularly at the central and provincial levels, was reduced. Superfluous organizations were abolished or merged with others. Steps were taken to eliminate much of the overlapping between the party and state bureaucracies.

Second, the Cultural Revolution saw a series of measures to

provide greater mass representation in political organizations. The recruitment policies of the party were changed to increase the access of workers and peasants to party membership. The revolutionary committees, in addition to military officers and veteran administrative cadres, also included ordinary workers or peasants serving as representatives of the masses. Their purpose was to ensure the responsiveness of decisions to local conditions and requirements, and, assuming the commitment of the masses to revolutionary values, to guarantee that any revisionist tendencies among the cadres would promptly be detected and corrected.

The establishment of the so-called "May 7th cadre schools" was a third important reform. Named after the date of a directive Mao issued in 1966, the May 7th schools offered a curriculum which combined ideological training, physical labor and close contact with ordinary workers and peasants. Most May 7th schools were located in rural areas, and the students joined local peasants in farming, land reclamation, water conservation and political discussion. Every cadre in China was supposed to spend six months to three years in a May 7th school, with one year the average course of study. And cadres are supposed to return to the schools periodically for refresher courses, to ensure that they do not become divorced from manual labor or from the masses.

As important as these reforms were, they did not represent the end of bureaucracy in China. Chinese political organizations after the Cultural Revolution remained hierarchical, with a formal division of labor, staffed largely by career bureaucrats. Even more important, some of the reforms appear to have had only limited effectiveness. The bureaucracy, temporarily reduced in size and complexity during the Cultural Revolution, has resumed its growth. Some organizations, for example, now have as many staff members as they did before the Cultural Revolution. The May 7th cadre schools functioned efficiently for a few years, but the Chinese press now reports that some cadres are finding excuses not to return for their second stint. While mass representatives still are members of the revolutionary committees, their power is slight, and the revolutionary committees as a whole have been eclipsed by the reconstructed party organization. Furthermore, the concept of direct mass representation has not been significantly reflected in the new party committees formed in the provinces.

These trends have received sharp criticism in the Chinese press recently, and attempts are being made to reverse them. In general, though, they demonstrate the degree to which the bureaucracy and the bureaucratic ethic survived the Cultural Revolution intact.

Higher Education

As Mao Tse-tung saw it, bureacratization was not the only potential source of revisionism in China. By the middle 1960's, Mao also began to have serious reservations about China's system of higher education and its effects on the values and attitudes of China's younger generation. Mao charged that neither the teaching staffs nor the curricula of China's colleges and universities had been sufficiently "revolutionized" since 1949. As a result, they were producing students who looked down on ordinary peasants and workers, disdained manual labor, and expected comfortable and influential positions in academia or the bureaucracy after graduation. In essence, Mao feared that both the bureaucracy and the universities were producing new elites: the bureaucracy, a group of career officials in their 30's, 40's and 50's; the universities, a generation of students in their early 20's. Both these elites, Mao believed, were increasingly divorced from the masses. Both sought material reward, social prominence and political power. Neither could be trusted to shun revisionism and continue following the revolutionary road.

Mao may also have suspected that there were direct connections—not simply similarities—between these two institutions. Obviously, many of the university students of the 1960's would become the bureaucrats of the 1970's, 80's and 90's and would carry the political attitudes learned in college with them to their official posts. In addition, many university students were the sons and daughters of China's present high officials. Because they had access to the best primary and secondary education in China,

TABLE I. *Estimated Economic Performance of Chin...*
Money in 1970 U.S. dollars

Period and year	GNP (billions of dollars)	Population, midyear (millions)	GNP per capita (dollars)	Industr product (1957 =
Rehabilitation				
1949	36	538	67	
1950	43	547	79	
1951	50	558	90	
1952	59	570	104	
First Five-Year Plan				
1953	63	583	108	
1954	66	596	110	
1955	72	611	117	
1956	78	626	124	
1957	82	642	128	1(
Great Leap Forward				
1958	95	658	144	1:
1959	92	674	137	1(
1960	89	689	130	161–1(
Readjustment and recovery				
1961	72	701	103	107–1
1962	79	710	112	108–1
1963	82	721	114	119–12
1964	90	735	122	133–14
1965	97	751	129	148–1(
Cultural Revolution				
1966	105	766	137	165–18
1967	101	783	129	134–14
1968	100	800	125	144–1(
1969	109	818	134	170–19
Resumption of regular planning				
1970	122	836	146	199–2
1971 [b]	128	855	150	223–

Source: Arthur G. Ashbrook, Jr., "China: Economic Policy anc
ment, A Compendium of Papers Submitted to the Joint Economic Co...
a. Negligible.
b. Preliminary

cultural duction (=100)	Steel output (millions of metric tons)	Grain output (millions of metric tons)	Foreign trade Volume (billions of dollars)	Percentage with Communist countries
54	0.16	108	0.83	
64	0.61	125	1.21	29
71	0.90	135	1.90	51
83	1.35	154	1.89	70
83	1.77	157	2.30	68
84	2.22	160	2.35	74
94	2.85	175	3.04	74
97	4.46	182	3.12	66
00	5.35	185	3.06	64
08	8.0	200	3.76	63
86	10.0	165	4.29	69
83	13.0	160	3.99	66
78	8.0	160	3.02	56
90	8.0	175–180	2.68	53
90	9.0	175–180	2.77	45
96	10.0	180–185	3.22	34
01	11.0	190–195	3.88	30
06	13.0	195–200	4.24	26
15	10.0	210–215	3.90	21
06	12.0	195–200	3.76	22
09	15.0	200–205	3.86	20
16	18.0	215–220	4.22	20
	21.0	215–220	4.50	21

ts, 1949–71," in *People's Republic of China: An Economic Assess-* ng. 2 sess. (1972), p. 5. Hereafter cited as *An Economic Assessment*.

and because of their family connections and the material benefits their parents could provide, they had a better chance than ordinary youth of entering China's most prestigious universities. Mao feared that China had produced a system of higher education in which one generation of officials could pass their rank and privileges on to their children.

In Mao's analysis, one particular shortcoming of China's student generations was that they had been born too late to experience the revolution personally. A 22-year old college student in 1965, for example, would have been only six years old when the Communists took power in 1949. One of the many goals of the Cultural Revolution, therefore, was to provide an environment in which Chinese youth could "make revolution." In mid-1966, universities throughout the country were closed to permit students to participate in the Red Guard movement. By rebelling against revisionist officials, the students would be able to acquire the same kind of revolutionary experience that Mao and his contemporaries had obtained through their struggles against the Manchu dynasty, the warlords and the Kuomintang. This intense, personal experience, Mao hoped, would strengthen their commitment to revolutionary goals and values.

Reform of Higher Education

As the most radical phase of the Cultural Revolution waned and the Red Guards were slowly disbanded, however, attention was shifted from the creation of a revolutionary environment to the reform of the higher educational system. After four years of intense debate and widespread experimentation, China's colleges and universities began to reopen in 1970 and 1971. One change was to revamp the curriculum, so as to ensure that students did not develop elitist attitudes toward manual labor, a spirit of competitiveness for good grades, or selfish desires for economic gain or political influence. To this end, Chinese universities today place greater emphasis on political study and manual labor than in the past. All textbooks and teaching materials have been revised, so that they embody Marxist analysis and Maoist values. Virtually all

Factory workers' appartments, Shanghai

Photos: Audrey Topping

Students helping on commune

teachers and professors—many of whom were educated abroad before 1949—have undergone intensive "reeducation." Most universities operate their own factories and farms, in which students perform regular manual labor. To ease competition for grades, exam questions are now circulated in advance, and students are allowed to consult their textbooks—and even their fellow students—during examinations.

The Chinese have also tried to eliminate the view that education offered a direct route into white-collar jobs. As a general rule, all middle-school and college graduates are sent to factories or communes after graduation. There, they not only perform manual labor but also serve as doctors, teachers, accountants, mechanics or technicians. High school graduates who want to enter college must spend two years in a factory or commune before they can apply; and even then they must receive the approval of their fellow workers or peasants. This policy has meant that there has been a vast flood of young people sent from urban high schools and colleges into the countryside over the past five years. While the exact figures are not available, some observers estimate that the total number of youth sent to the countryside approaches 20 million.

Finally, the Cultural Revolution also saw significant changes in university admissions policy. To ensure that youth from worker and peasant backgrounds had a greater chance to attend college, more emphasis was placed on the class background and political attitudes of applicants than on their formal academic qualifications. In addition, the Chinese have made arrangements for older workers and peasants without high school training to attend university courses. The goal, the Chinese have said, is to make sure that university enrollments reflect more accurately the class structure of Chinese society.

Criticisms of the Reforms

Taken together, these reforms represent an effort to provide a revolutionary education for China's university students—to ensure that they are committed to revolutionary goals, that they are willing to engage in manual labor, that their skills are suited to the country's economic needs and that they do not represent a potential revisionist elite drawn only from the urban, well-to-do classes. Interestingly, however, the restructuring of the system of higher education was one of the first Cultural Revolution reforms to come under open criticism in the early 1970's. Many youth, particularly Red Guards, who were forced to leave the cities for the countryside, complained that they had been sent into a kind of political exile and that they were not being able to apply the skills they had learned in middle-school and college. Many peasants and rural cadres, too, resented the influx of urban youth into the communes. Many discontented youths returned secretly to the cities, where, without valid grain ration coupons, they had to engage in street crime to support themselves. One observer has estimated that there may be as many as 50,000 youth living illegally in Peking alone.

The increase in urban crime and in the number of youth escaping to the cities was only one consequence of the Cultural Revolution's policies toward youth and education. Another was growing criticism from professors and university administrators that the modifications of the curriculum had seriously lowered the quality of Chinese higher education, and that the emphasis on political admissions criteria to the neglect of academic standards was permitting unqualified students to enter the universities. Such a system might produce mechanics and technicians, they admitted. But how could it meet China's demands for highly skilled scientists and engineers?

Largely in response to these criticisms, some of the Cultural Revolution reforms were quietly relaxed in 1972 and 1973. Examinations were reinstituted as part of the university admissions process. Professors began stressing the academic, as well as the political, content of their courses. Highly qualified students from bourgeois families were assured that despite their class background, they too had a place in Chinese universities. Some students with special abilities in the sciences and the arts were allowed to proceed directly from middle school to college, or from college to graduate school, without the usual period of manual labor. And some cadres began using their influence to gain their children college admissions, or to save them from being sent to remote rural areas after their graduation from middle school.

Almost immediately, these changes aroused serious opposition from two groups: youth of worker-peasant origins, but with poor academic qualifications, who suspected that the doors to university education were again being closed to them; and radical political leaders, who were concerned about the dangers of revisionism in China. Both groups feared that the Cultural Revolution was gradually being undone and the educational system was being permitted to return to its pre-Cultural Revolutionary state. By late 1973, education had once again become one of the central issues in Chinese politics, as Chinese leaders debated the importance of "continuing the revolution" in education.

Implications for the Future

Has Mao achieved his goal of institutionalizing the revolution in China? Will Maoism remain the guiding ideological force in China in the years ahead, or will revisionist tendencies begin to reappear? What will be the fate of the Maoist vision in a post-Maoist China?

No one can be certain, of course, but there are some tentative answers that seem plausible. On the positive side, Maoism has clearly identified some of the major social tensions that arise during the process of modernization: the emergence of inequalities between bureaucrats and their constituents, between skilled and unskilled workers, between city and countryside, and between the areas that enjoy the benefits of economic progress and those that do not. The basic premise of Maoism—that development should not be permitted to produce undue unequality—is a compelling one and is likely to have widespread appeal to the disadvantaged sectors of Chinese society.

On the other hand, Mao's death will reduce the influence of

his ideology in two important ways. First, Chinese leaders will soon discover that Mao's writings, because of their complexity and ambiguity, can be interpreted in innumerable ways, and appropriate passages can be found to justify both sides in virtually any policy dispute. Without Mao present to clarify the ambiguities, to resolve disagreements over interpretation and explain the significance of his ideology for the problems at hand, Maoism may begin to decay into a set of ritualized slogans and clichés, used on ceremonial occasions to justify decisions actually reached on pragmatic grounds.

Perhaps more important, Maoist views of development have never received unanimous support among Chinese leaders. Even in the 1950's, and to a great extent in the early 1960's, many of Mao's colleagues opposed the policies he advocated, particularly his consistent emphasis on class struggle and on minimizing inequality in the course of modernization. It took Mao's own personal prestige and political skills, as well as the support his ideology enjoyed among China's students and less-skilled workers, to launch the Cultural Revolution in the face of such opposition. After Mao dies, it is highly unlikely that other leaders will emerge who combine his commitment to revolutionary values and his ability to mobilize enough political support to see them implemented.

The most probable outcome, therefore, is that Maoism will neither die or flourish. It will continue to attract substantial support, but will never again have the political impact it enjoyed during Mao's lifetime. It will gradually be distorted and corrupted, as Mao's successors reinterpret it to justify their policies. And it will increasingly fall victim to the pressures toward pragmatization and specialization in policy-making. Maoism may well become a perpetual counterculture in post-Maoist China: able to criticize the trends toward bureaucratization, routinization and inequality that accompany modernization, but unable to halt them.

Political Institutions
and Leadership

Perhaps the most important factor in the succession will be the kind of political institutions and political leadership that China has at the time of Mao's death. To weather the succession smoothly, China will need a collective leadership that is representative of all the major groups and interests in Chinese political life, and yet one that can compromise its internal differences and avoid serious political conflict. China will also need a stable institutional structure that can provide continuity and legitimacy to the new post-Maoist leadership. Conversely, an unclear set of institutional arrangements, or a leadership wracked by internal conflict, will tend to make the succession a long and unsettled process.

In this respect, the Cultural Revolution and its aftermath did much to complicate the succession. The purges of Liu Shao-ch'i and Lin Piao created a leadership vacuum and shook the institutional structure of the entire Chinese regime. Both the party and the government saw some of their highest officials dismissed or transferred, their normal routines suspended, their organizational tables scrapped and their legitimacy in society questioned. The army temporarily assumed an abnormally important role in Chinese politics, but its more permanent relations with the other major political institutions remained controversial.

After the purge of Lin, Chou En-lai assumed the responsibility for reconstructing China's political institutions and assembling a central collective leadership that could survive the death of Mao. Chou's skills in political bargaining and compromise, his personal prestige and his reputation as a pragmatic Maoist seemed to make him uniquely qualified for this task. Nonetheless, despite some significant accomplishments, the poor state of Chou's health and opposition from more radical leaders have raised doubts about Chou's ability to manage the succession successfully.

The Military

One of the most important outcomes of the Cultural Revolution was the assumption by the military of a preeminent position in the Chinese political process. With competing Red Guard organizations pushing the country's major cities near anarchy, the PLA provided Peking with an essential instrument for restoring social order. And with both the party and government bureaucracies in disarray, the army alone possessed the manpower and the discipline to transmit central directives to the provinces and ensure their implementation.

As a result, when the rebuilding of the party began with the convening of the Ninth Party Congress in April 1969, the military dominated the process. The most obvious symbol of the military's new status in China was the election of Lin Piao as sole party vice-chairman and successor to Mao. But the influence of the military was also reflected in the composition of the central party organs elected at the congress. Of the 25-man Politburo, nearly half were military men; 45 percent of the 279 positions on the Central Committee were occupied by military cadres, compared to 19 percent of the seats on the previous Central Committee elected in 1956.

Military participation was equally evident in the new provincial party committees formed between 1969 and 1971. In 20 of China's 29 provinces, the first party secretary was a military man. And if all 158 provincial party secretaries are considered—not just the 29 first secretaries—we find that PLA cadres constituted 59 percent of the total.

By mid-1971, then, the PLA had assumed a position in civilian politics unknown since the regional military governments of the early 1950's were transformed into civilian rule. The extent of military influence profoundly disturbed many civilian leaders. While Mao had been willing to order military intervention in the Cultural Revolution in January 1967, he apparently felt that institutionalization of military participation in civilian affairs threatened the concept of civilian control of the military. Nominally, local PLA units were subordinate to the provincial party committees, and the entire PLA was subject to the control of the party Politburo and its Military Affairs Committee. But if the army simultaneously occupied so many key seats on the Politburo and in the provinces, how effective could this "civilian" control be? Would this not contradict Mao's principle that "the party must command the gun"?

Still another cause for concern was Lin Piao's policy of appointing his own associates to key military and party positions. The idea of an independent military was bad enough. But the spectre of a private army, organized on the basis of personal loyalty to its commander and his subordinates, was too reminiscent of the warlord forces of the 1910's and 20's to be acceptable to most Chinese leaders.

Curbing the Military

After Lin's purge, therefore, Chinese civilian leaders—moderates and radicals alike—quickly began to dismantle the vestiges of his patronage network within the PLA. The first step was to eliminate Lin's associates from their positions on the Politburo and in the central military commands. To deal with Lin's

Cadre school for officials

provincial supporters, Peking had to proceed more cautiously, for many had been able to construct strong local power bases. Nonetheless, the trend in the provinces, as in Peking, has been to replace men closely associated with Lin with officers who had fewer personal ties with the former defense minister.

With Lin's followers purged, transferred or counterbalanced by other appointments, Chou—again with radical support—began to curb the role of the military in Chinese politics more generally. Just as the Ninth Party Congress in 1969 symbolized the rise of the military, so did the Tenth Congress in August 1973 mark the reassertion of civilian control. The proportion of Central Committee seats occupied by PLA cadres fell from 45 percent in 1969 to 32 percent in 1973. Even more important, only four full members of the present Politburo are active-duty military officers, compared to ten in 1969.

By late 1973 the one remaining symbol of military influence was the status of China's 11 regional military commanders. Two of the eleven had been named to the Politburo in 1969 (and continued to serve on the new Politburo elected in August 1973); and virtually all were either first or second party secretaries in one of the provinces under their jurisdiction. Some had served in their posts for more than 15 years and had established networks of close personal relationships with both military subordinates and civilian colleagues. The combination of the central power of some and the local power of all raised serious questions about their ultimate responsiveness to central civilian control.

That this power had to be curbed, civilian officials in Peking could agree. But any attempt to reduce their influence would have to be undertaken with the utmost care, for they were too powerful to be dismissed *en masse*. Chou's solution to this dilemma, implemented in late 1973, was a carefully orchestrated rotation of these key officers, in which nine of the eleven were reassigned to other regional commands. While none was formally demoted, those who were transferred lost both their provincial party secretaryships and their informal local contacts in the process. But since none obviously benefited at the expense of the others, all were willing to acquiesce to the transfers.

What has been the result of these attempts to reassert civilian control over the Chinese military? Without question, the role of PLA officers in civilian decision-making has been substantially reduced. But civilian control over the PLA is still not as tight as it was before the Cultural Revolution. Moreover, the potential for a revival of military influence still exists, particularly if China should experience political disorder at the time of the succession. The Cultural Revolution may have set a precedent for future military intervention in Chinese civilian politics.

The Party

China is one of the most highly organized societies in the world. Virtually every Chinese is a member of at least one formal organization—an urban neighborhood association, a rural production team, a work group in a factory or office, the party, the militia, the army, a trade union, the Communist Youth League, the Women's Federation—and some are members of as many as three or four. But of this vast array of organizations, the party is the most important. According to the party constitution, all other organizations are to "accept the leadership of the party." To exercise this leadership, party members occupy the leading positions in the army, the state bureaucracy, the communes and the mass organizations, where they ensure the implementation of party policies. Party members who do not hold official positions in other organizations—the vast majority of the party's 28 million members —are supposed to serve as models of efficiency, discipline and commitment for their fellow workers, and thereby convey party policy to the masses in less formal ways.

By the middle 1960's, however, Mao Tse-tung had come to believe that the party was misusing its leadership position. Mao feared that the party was quickly becoming an entrenched, unresponsive, overstaffed and elitist organization. While Mao never wanted to eliminate the party as an organization, or abandon the concept of party leadership, he did want to shake up the party, to make it more ideologically pure, more efficient and more responsive to local conditions. The reinvigoration of the party, then, was one of the principal aims of the Cultural Revolution.

The immediate result of the Cultural Revolution, however, was not to strengthen the party but to weaken it. The nationwide purges of party leaders effectively disbanded the party organization; and the army, the Red Guards and other revolutionary organizations won considerable autonomy from party control.

Since the end of the Cultural Revolution in 1969, the party has slowly been reconstructed. New central party organs—a Central Committee, a Politburo and a Politburo Standing Committee —were elected at the two party congresses held in 1969 and 1973. New provincial and local party committees have been formed to replace those disbanded during the Cultural Revolution. Recruitment to the party has been resumed, and the party membership rolls have been substantially enlarged. While the party's relationship with the PLA is still somewhat ambiguous, the party has acquired much closer control over the state bureaucracy than it enjoyed before the Cultural Revolution.

Cleavages in the Party

Despite China's recent successes in rebuilding it, the party is still not a homogeneous institution. At least three important cleavages continue to divide its ranks. One such cleavage arises from the disagreements held by radicals and moderates over a broad range of policy issues. While, as we have indicated, the basic contours of China's agricultural policy are not as controversial as they once were, there remain substantial differences over foreign and educational policy, as well as the possibility of renewed debate over strategies of industrial development and the distribution of social services.

A second cleavage separates the central party organization in Peking and the 29 provincial committees. One significant result of the Cultural Revolution has been the growing importance of provincial leaders within the party. In part, this was due to the policies of economic decentralization adopted during the Cultural Revolution. But it also occurred because many of the provincial leaders who emerged during the late 1960's had strong personal power bases in the provincial party and government bureaucracies, in local military units or in local mass organizations, and thus were not completely beholden to Peking for their appointments. In some cases, Peking could only ratify the appointment of men who had gained the upper hand in local power struggles.

The rise of these provincial leaders can be seen most clearly in the composition of the Central Committee. The Eighth Central Committee, elected in 1956, was composed primarily of national leaders working in Peking. Only 38 percent of this committee were provincial officials. At the Ninth Party Congress in 1969, these figures were completely reversed: only 33 percent of the Ninth

Central Committee were central leaders, while 67 percent came from the provinces. This same 2-to-1 ratio in favor of provincial officials was roughly maintained in the Tenth Central Committee elected in August 1973.

Experts disagree as to the implications of this trend for central-provincial relations in China. Some point to the apparent ability of provincial leaders to implement central directives in a discretionary manner and argue that central control over the provincial party committees has been weakened. Others, however, respond that the Politburo clearly retains the power to purge or transfer local leaders who step too far out of line and point to the recent rotation of China's military region commanders as evidence. All agree, however, that the party apparatus in China today is much less centralized than it was in the 1950's.

Experts are also uncertain as to how much disagreement there is among China's provincial leaders. Most observers assume, however, that the outlook of provincial party secretaries varies from province to province. The leaders of industrial Heilungkiang, remote Sinkiang, agrarian Hupeh and urban Shanghai probably differ substantially in their views on major policy issues—just as the governors of Pennsylvania, Alaska, Kansas and the mayor of New York do in the United States. Because these provincial leaders have increased access to central decision-making bodies, policy-making in China may well be characterized by increasing conflict among divergent provincial interests.

A third cleavage that is now emerging in the party is a generational one. The rapid expansion of the party—from about 4.5 million members in 1949 to about 20 million before the Cultural Revolution and 28 million today—brought large numbers of younger men and women into the party. Those under 40 probably constitute, as a conservative estimate, about 50 percent of Party membership. But while younger people swelled the party rank-and-file, veteran party cadres continued to monopolize both central and provincial leadership positions. Throughout the party organization, younger men and women had little opportunity for advancement. This situation obviously aroused the resentment of the younger cadres. And it also created concern among some older leaders, who felt that party decision-making councils could benefit from the drive and enthusiasm of younger people.

One announced reform of the Cultural Revolution, therefore, was to "take in fresh blood," as Mao put it, by increasing the participation of younger generations in party decision-making. In 1970 the party adopted the principle that party committees at all levels, including the center and the provinces, should be a "three-in-one combination" of old (over 60), middle-aged (40-60) and young (20-40) cadres. An important symbol of this policy was the election of two younger men to the Politburo: Yao Wen-yüan, a Shanghai propagandist, joined the Politburo in 1969 at the age of 38; and Wang Hung-wen, a former Shanghai textile factory worker and leader of the Shanghai workers' movement during the Cultural Revolution, was promoted to a party vice-chairmanship in 1973, also at the age of 38.

In general, however, the "three-in-one combination" was not vigorously implemented. For one thing, nothing was said explicitly about the proportions in which positions should be allocated among the old, the middle-aged and the young. In few local party committees have people under 40 been given one-third of the seats. In fact, the trend has been the rehabilitation of "veteran cadres" purged during the Cultural Revolution, most of whom are in their 60's.

Even in the central party apparatus—the elections of Yao and Wang aside—the effects of the policy have been slight. The average age of the full members of the Central Committee is about 63, and more than 75 percent are over 60. Despite the presence of Yao and Wang, the average age of Politburo members is now more than 66.

In short, China has not yet been able to make significant progress in bringing younger people into leading positions in the party. And recent complaints by younger cadres like Wang that the party is still wedded to the principle of seniority indicate that the generation gap remains wide.

Mass Organizations

Of all the organizational networks in China, the system of mass organizations—the trade unions, the Communist Youth League, the Women's Federation, the peasant associations and the militia—is the most extensive. Like the party, these organizations were seriously disrupted during the Cultural Revolution. For a time, their place was taken by the Red Guards and other "revolutionary rebel" groups. But as the Cultural Revolution came to an end, and the turbulent Red Guard organizations disbanded, China began to rebuild its elaborate system of formal mass organizations.

This task, too, has been marked by controversy, for Chinese leaders concerned with mass organization work cannot seem to agree on what the proper role of post-Cultural Revolutionary mass organizations should be. When reconstruction of the mass organizations began in the early 1970's, three competing organizational models were available. The first was the traditional Leninist model: the mass organizations served as a "transmission belt" for carrying party policy to the nonparty masses and for ensuring that public opinion would flow in orderly ways to the party elite. The second was a kind of pressure group model: the mass organizations articulated and sponsored the economic and social interests of their members within party decision-making councils. While not sanctioned by Leninist doctrine, this function had been actively performed by some mass organizations—especially the trade unions—during the early 1960's. Finally, there was the Red Guard model: the mass organizations, relatively independent of party control, could allow the nonparty masses to criticize party officials for making decisions that violated Maoist doctrine.

Since the Cultural Revolution, virtually all Chinese leaders have rejected the pressure group model, on the grounds that it sought economic advantages for the few instead of pursuing the broader interests of society as a whole. But there has been widespread debate over the relative merits of the transmission belt and Red Guard models. In general, the radicals have seen the mass organizations as a potential political resource, to be used in future power struggles and policy debates with the moderates. In supporting the Red Guard model, they have therefore sought to keep the mass organizations relatively independent from party control and have argued that the mass organizations should retain the right to criticize party policy when it departs from Maoist principles. More moderate leaders, fearing a replay of the Cultural Revolution, have attempted to bring the mass organizations under tighter party discipline. They tend, that is, to support the transmission belt model in mass organization work.

The outcome of this debate is still not clear. While it appears that the moderates retain the upper hand, radical leaders have been able to gain important positions in some mass organizations, particularly the urban militia and some urban trade councils. There remains the possibility, therefore, that the mass organizations may again provide an independent power base for radical leaders engaging in political struggle in China.

China's Collective Leadership

One important conclusion that emerges from this discussion is that, despite the commonly held view that China is a monolithic society, Chinese politics is characterized by a substantial degree of pluralism. The Chinese political system since the Cultural Revolution has been marked by tensions and cleavages among the party, the army and the mass organizations; between provincial and central leaders; between young cadres and their older superiors; and between moderates and radicals. A smooth succession seems to require the formation of a collective leadership in which all these competing interests are represented, and which has enough mutual trust and respect to permit the conciliation and compromise of conflicting views.

The central party leadership selected at the Tenth Congress in August 1973 represents Chou En-lai's effort to create such a balance. The congress elected a 25-member Politburo (which added an additional member in early 1974), that meets probably once or twice a month to formulate basic party policies; a smaller, 9-man Standing Committee, that meets more frequently to consider problems arising between regular Politburo meetings; and a 319-man Central Committee, that may meet every other year or so to discuss and ratify Politburo decisions.

Of these, the Politburo is the most powerful body—and also best reflects the composition of China's present leadership. The identification of factions within the Politburo is an extremely difficult task for outsiders to undertake, and Western observers differ considerably in their detailed analyses of China's leadership. But most experts do agree on several crucial points. First, the Politburo is divided along ideological lines between a radical faction, apparently led by Mao's wife Chiang Ch'ing and the young propagandist Yao Wen-yüan, and a more moderate faction, headed by Premier Chou En-lai. The exact size and composition of these two groups is not clearly known, but it does seem that only a minority of the Politburo is firmly committed to either. Second, Mao Tse-tung appears to respect the contributions of both groups to Chinese political life, believing that the moderates possess the administrative skills essential to the orderly and effective implementation of policy, and that the radicals are necessary to maintain commitment to the ideals of the Cultural Revolution. Accordingly, Mao has seemed to shift his support periodically between the radicals and the moderates, to ensure that neither group is able to gain dominance over the other.

Perhaps most important, the Politburo is broadly representative of the most significant groups and institutions in Chinese politics. Its 26 members include spokesmen for both radical and moderate policy positions. It has representatives of peasants, workers, national minorities, women and the young. It draws its membership from the provinces as well as the center, from the PLA as well as the civilian bureaucracies and from the mass organizations. But, in reflecting the diversity of Chinese politics, the Politburo is also deeply divided. It remains to be seen whether this collective leadership can work together in harmony during the transition process.

Implications for the Succession

In the past several years, China has made considerable progress in rebuilding the political institutions shattered during the Cultural Revolution. But despite the undeniable progress, some substantial problems remain.

First of all, the purge of Lin Piao and his supporters in 1971-72, and the mass transfer of regional military commanders in late 1973, have created important vacancies at both the central and provincial levels which have not yet been filled. As of mid-June 1974, for instance, nine provinces had no first party secretary; the PLA had no minister of defense, no chief of staff and no head of logistics; and several cabinet-level departments had no ministers.

Moreover, although they have repeatedly promised to do so, the Chinese have not yet convened a National People's Congress—China's highest legislative body—to adopt a new constitution and complete the reform of the state bureaucracy. This suggests that there is controversy over appointments to key ministries and vice-premierships, and continuing uncertainty as to whether to maintain or abolish the position of state chairman, previously held by Liu Shao-ch'i and sought so actively by Lin Piao.

At the beginning of this chapter, we indicated that China would need a clear and stable set of political institutions, and a representative and unified collective leadership, in order to effect a smooth transition to a post-Maoist era. Not all these conditions have been met. Although the party has been rebuilt and the principle of party leadership has been reasserted, the relationships between the party and the army, the party and the mass organizations, and the party and the state, all remain ambiguous. The division of responsibilities between Peking and the provinces has not yet been clearly defined. And, perhaps most important, China's new collective leadership seems deeply divided along ideological lines. In institutional terms, at least, the possibility of a troubled succession still exists.

The Uncertain Future

China is now engaged in its third attempt to resolve the complex problem of the succession to Mao. Since the purge of Lin Piao in 1971, Chou En-lai has attempted to reconstruct a stable set of political institutions, assemble a broadly based collective leadership and create a consensus around his foreign and domestic policies in the hope of avoiding the reemergence of serious political conflict before Mao's death. Until recently, observers had been hopeful that Chou's political skills would enable him to complete the task successfully and that he could lead China smoothly through the critical months that will follow the death of the chairman. The events of the past year, however, have raised serious doubts about the eventual success of Chou's efforts, as his health deteriorated and conflict intensified between China's radical and moderate leaders.

The Moderates Under Fire

Since the summer of 1973, some of China's foreign and domestic policies, and some of its national and provincial leaders, have come under severe criticism from radicals dissatisfied with China's course since the Cultural Revolution. The radicals initially expressed their views in a form that may seem peculiar to Westerners, but one that is characteristic of much public political dialogue in China. Rather than attack their opponents directly, the radicals concentrated their fire on the ancient Chinese philosopher Confucius, a man who has been dead for more than 2000 years. But the evidence indicates that the principal target of this "anti-Confucius" campaign was much less the ancient sage than a more modern mandarin: Chou En-lai himself.

The campaign against Confucius began modestly enough in late 1972 with the appearance of a rather scholarly article, written by a professor of history in Canton, accusing Confucius of being a reactionary rather than a progressive force in Chinese history. From that point, the campaign gradually gathered momentum as other writers first denounced the political philosophy of Confucius and his disciples, and then analyzed the historical significance of a wide range of other emperors, officials and philosophers. To be sure, some of the campaign was genuinely directed at the vestiges of Confucianism in Chinese political and social life, particularly since the Confucian advocacy of authoritarian rule by a scholar-elite, disdain for manual labor and emphasis on social harmony all conflict with Chinese Communist concepts of proletarian revolution, equality and struggle. But much of the campaign used complicated historical analogies to criticize Chou En-lai, his handling of the succession and the policies he has sponsored since the Cultural Revolution.

Reading between the lines of the long, dry, detailed "historical" commentaries appearing in the Chinese press, Western observers have concluded that the radicals have opposed Chou for three principal reasons. The first is Chou's foreign policy, particularly his sponsorship of détente with the United States, his seemingly lukewarm support for revolutionary movements in the third world and his advocacy of increased trade and cultural exchanges with the West. (We will consider this issue in greater detail shortly.)

Second, the radicals have been dissatisfied with the way in which Chou has been reconstructing China's political structure and have been especially concerned about his policies toward cadres and mass organizations. Criticisms of Confucius for seeking to "restore old families" deposed from the aristocracy and for "calling back to office those who had retired into obscurity" were only slightly disguised complaints that Chou has been sponsoring the rehabilitation of veteran party cadres criticized and dismissed during the Cultural Revolution instead of replacing them with younger, more radical candidates. Similarly, accusations that Confucius wanted "the slaves to be loyal to the slave-owners," and that he advocated unquestioning obedience to officials, almost certainly refer to Chou's efforts to bring the resurrected mass organizations firmly under party control.

Third and perhaps most important, the radicals have clearly opposed the general thrust of domestic policy since 1971, particularly in the educational and cultural spheres. The reinstatement of college entrance examinations, the gradual reappearance of inefficiency and even corruption in the bureaucracy, and the production of some plays and operas said to be critical of Mao and his policies have led the radicals to conclude that Chou has allowed the present period of moderation to proceed much too far. They have accused Chou of having opposed the Cultural Revolution from the beginning (a charge which is probably partially correct, for while sympathetic to some of Mao's policy aims, he did not approve of the violence and anarchism of the Red Guard movement), of slighting its accomplishments and of encouraging the gradual abandonment of some of its reforms. Like Confucius, Chou is said to have "opposed social change" and to have favored "retrogression" to less progressive programs.

From Chou, the radicals turned to other targets. They encouraged factory and office workers in Peking and the provincial capitals to write wall posters criticizing the policies and behavior of party and government cadres. Beginning in June 1974, China experienced a lively wall poster campaign, somewhat reminiscent of the early months of the Cultural Revolution, in which cadres responsible for factory management and municipal and provincial administration were charged with corruption, reversing the reforms of the Cultural Revolution and suppressing mass criticism of their policies.

Chou's Response

Chou's response to these charges combined elements of both retreat and counterattack. Chou began by compromising with the radicals on several important issues. In his speech to the Tenth Party Congress, he pointedly defended and praised the accomplishments of the Cultural Revolution and implied that he would not permit any further attempts to reverse them. The composition of the new central party leadership also contained several concessions to the radicals: the election of a large contingent of leftists to the Politburo, the promotion of Wang Hung-wen to the third-ranking position in the party and the appointment of three mass representatives as Politburo members. In foreign policy, relations with the United States cooled, and Chou began expressing stronger and more frequent support for third world revolutionary movements.

Even as he compromised with the radicals on some issues, however, Chou fought to bring the "anti-Confucius" and wall poster campaigns under tighter control. First, he skillfully shifted the focus of the anti-Confucius campaign from his own policies to those of the discredited Lin Piao. With Mao's apparent acquiescence, he convinced the Politburo that the radicals should not be permitted to form any revolutionary mass organizations, such as the Red Guards, which would be independent of local party leadership. He largely defused the wall poster campaign by insisting that local party committees be empowered to "correct any incorrect ideas'' the masses might express. He filled the press with calls for unity and discipline. And finally, in early July, the Politburo directed that the radicals' campaigns should not be allowed to interfere with agricultural or industrial production.

By early August, in short, Chou and the moderates had begun to place significant limits on the radicals' freedom of political action. But radical criticism of Chou and his policies could still be seen in the Chinese press, and a complete moderate victory was by no means assured.

Moreover, in the midst of his struggle with the radicals, Chou was also forced to contend with his own failing health. In early July, it was learned that Chou had been hospitalized with a serious heart attack. After a brief public appearance at the end of the month, he returned to the hospital amid reports that his condition had worsened. Although Chinese officials insisted that Chou continued to perform his principal duties as premier, Vice-Premiers Teng Hsiao-p'ing and Li Hsien-nien began to substitute for Chou in attending meetings and receptions for visiting foreign dignitaries. It was obvious that Chou's age (76) and the grueling pace he had maintained ever since the beginning of the Cultural Revolution (18-hour days) had finally taken their toll.

As of this writing, the state of Chou's health and the final outcome of his struggle with the radicals remain unclear. But the spectre suddenly appeared that China might have to weather the transition without him. The fate of Chou's carefully constructed succession arrangements, which many considered the key to political stability, hung in the balance.

Factors Shaping the Succession

Four factors will shape the forthcoming succession in China: the legacy of past attempts to arrange the succession; the degree of disagreement over China's basic social, economic and foreign policies; China's ability to rebuild a stable institutional structure that could survive Mao's death; and the presence of a leader like

Chou with the skills and prestige to help resolve the problems that will inevitably arise during the transition. With these factors in mind, a brief review of our conclusions thus far clearly indicates why there is such a sense of uncertainty surrounding the succession. First, the purges of Lin and Liu demonstrated that no succession arrangement is necessarily final and that violence, intrigue, the invocation of military force and the mobilization of mass support outside institutional channels are all tactics which Chinese leaders may employ in the pursuit of power. Second, while there seems to be widespread consensus on most aspects of economic policy, serious disagreement could easily emerge if China experiences any economic difficulties. Mao's campaign to revitalize the bureaucracy appears to have had only partial success, and many leaders clearly oppose further attempts to "continue the revolution" through massive disruptions of organizational routine. Educational policy, too, remains controversial, with the fate of the reforms conducted during the Cultural Revolution still undetermined. Third, China's institutional structure, while largely rebuilt since the Cultural Revolution, remains ambiguous and incomplete in certain key areas; and the new collective leadership, while broadly representative of competing interests, is obviously plagued by disagreements and divisions. Finally, Chou's poor health and the opposition he has aroused among some Chinese leaders have threatened his ability to manage the succession upon Mao's death.

For all these reasons, the prediction of China's future after Mao is extremely difficult. Rather than attempt to make a single "best guess" about what will happen after Mao dies, it is better to think in terms of the possible alternatives and to consider under what circumstances each alternative might actually come about. When we do so, we realize that China faces no less than three possible futures: a smooth succession, characterized by compromise between moderates and radicals; a more turbulent succession, marked by a swing toward greater radicalism, and a stalemated succession, possibly characterized by serious political disorder. How might each of these scenarios occur?

Scenario for a Smooth Succession

The first possible future envisions an essentially smooth succession, with the collective leadership formed at the Tenth Party Congress continuing unchanged into the post-Maoist era. While a new party chairman would be elected after Mao's death, almost certainly from among the present members of the Politburo, he would primarily be a symbol of national unity and would rule only after considerable consultation with his Politburo colleagues. This collective leadership would continue to have their disagreements, but, in large part out of a commitment to maintaining national unity through a difficult transition, they would not permit these differences to descend into open conflict. In general, therefore, this collective leadership would continue the broad outlines of China's current domestic and foreign policies, although possibly with some minor adjustments in educational and cultural policy to win the support of the radicals.

If this scenario is to occur, several conditions will have to be met. First, Chou must be able to forestall or block any further radical attacks on his policies. He must convince most radicals that the trend toward moderation since the Cultural Revolution has been halted and that he is willing to make concessions on the issues about which they are most deeply concerned. His policies must continue to be effective in meeting China's foreign and domestic goals; he must avoid any setbacks which might cost him further support within the Politburo. Finally, and most important, Chou must not lose Mao's confidence. He must continue to demonstrate his loyalty to Mao's principles and avoid any appearance that, like Lin Piao, he seeks ultimate power in China even before Mao's death.

So far, Chou seems to have been able to meet these conditions reasonably well. But what if Chou should die before Mao? While not eliminating the possibility of a smooth succession, Chou's death would certainly reduce it. No other member of the Politburo has Chou's experience, contacts, political skills or prestige. Chou's most likely successor as premier, Vice Premier Teng Hsiao-p'ing, was accused of being Liu Shao-ch'i's principal supporter during the Cultural Revolution and returned to office only in early 1973. While Teng is an experienced administrator, it is doubtful that he would enjoy the same degree of political support as Chou or that he could manage the succession as skillfully.

Scenario for a Radical Succession

In China's second possible future, the current radical challenge would continue, gradually gain support from previously uncommitted leaders and ultimately win majority support on the Politburo. The radicals would then be in a position to purge some of the moderates now occupying key positions in China—possibly even Chou himself—and could gain the acquiescence of others to more radical domestic and foreign policies.

This second scenario essentially assumes a set of conditions opposite to the first. It assumes that the radicals are neither satisfied with the compromises that Chou has been willing to make, nor deterred by the support he now seems to have in the Politburo. Instead, the radicals bide their time, waiting for the moderates' policies to fail and looking for opportunities to win over wavering members of the Politburo. The reemergence of bureaucratic inefficiency, signs of slackening ideological commitment among youth, evidence of "revisionism" in intellectual life, growing inequalities in the economy, a serious crop failure or a crisis in China's foreign relations could reduce the credibility of the moderates and increase the influence of the radicals. During Mao's lifetime, the radicals' aim would be to use such problems and setbacks to win the chairman's support away from China's present policies and leadership.

But two difficult questions remain. First, what is Mao's view of the political trends in China since the Cultural Revolution? At what point might he decide to support the radicals in an all-out attack on China's more moderate leaders? How much confidence does Mao place in Chou? Unfortunately, no one outside China can answer these crucial questions. Mao has published no major essays in recent years, granted no interviews and made few speeches. His part in recent developments—and the role he might choose to play in the future—remain mysteries to Western observers.

Second, could the radicals mount a successful challenge to China's present leaders without Mao alive to support them? At a minimum, a successful radical offensive after Mao's death would require substantial backing from the PLA, and widespread dissatisfaction among China's provincial leaders. The excesses of the Cultural Revolution cost China's radicals much support, and their political influence will probably decrease further upon Mao's death. While China after Mao may still see periods of radical politics, most observers believe that the probability of radical rule in the post-Maoist era will be substantially reduced.

Scenario for Stalemate

China's third possible future envisions a deadlock between moderates and radicals on the Politburo after Mao's death due to an inability to agree on the composition of post-Maoist leadership or the direction of post-Maoist policies. From here, this scenario could evolve in different directions. One result of deadlock at the center might simply be the tacit acceptance of substantial provincial autonomy, as occurred in China in the 1910's and 20's. A more disturbing possibility, however, is that the two factions might be willing to risk political turmoil for the sake of power and try to break the stalemate by appealing to groups outside the party for assistance. The radicals, for example, might follow Mao's lead and seek to mobilize mass support; while the moderates might try to gain the backing of the military commanders. A willingness to carry the struggle outside the established institutional framework would certainly produce serious social disorder, just as the Cultural Revolution did. Ultimately, because of its control of armed force, the PLA would probably prevail, and China would experience a period of thinly disguised military rule.

69

The Succession and Chinese Foreign Policy

In their attempts to formulate an effective foreign policy since 1949, Chinese leaders have been particularly concerned with finding solutions to three central questions. First, what foreign policy posture is most compatible with China's domestic social and economic goals? Second, how can China help foster a revolutionary transformation of the international system in favor of poorer peoples and nations around the world? And, most important, how can China ensure its own security against the nations it believes to be the major status-quo powers: the United States and, since the mid-1960's, the Soviet Union? China's policy since the Cultural Revolution, formulated largely by Chou En-lai, has been a fresh attempt to cope with these three problems and has probably been China's most effective international posture to date.

Under Chou, China's strategy for promoting a revolution in the international system has differed considerably from that of the past. Rather than emphasize support of revolutionary movements inside third world countries—a policy China adopted at times in the 1950's and, to a lesser extent, in the early 1960's—China now advocates the formation of an alliance of virtually all established third world governments against the political and economic "domination" of the superpowers. China is encouraging the third world to assert control over its natural resources, to raise the prices of its raw material exports and to improve the terms of its economic dealings with the superpowers and the multinational corporations. The Chinese also point out that Eastern Europe, Western Europe and Japan also have political and economic disagreements with the United States and the Soviet Union and are thus potential partners in the worldwide alliance against the superpowers. China believes that the isolation of the United States and the Soviet Union in the world arena will greatly enhance the prospects for a restructuring of international political and economic relationships.

Security Problems

When considering more immediate security problems, however,

Peking summit: (l. to r.) Chou En-lai, interpreter, Mao, Nixon, Kissinger

Audrey Topping

China's prime minister, Chou En-lai

the Chinese have taken a somewhat different approach. The most crucial threat to Chinese security since 1967 has been the massive build-up of Soviet forces along the Chinese border, which led to serious Sino-Soviet border clashes in 1969. Although the Russians consistently deny any hostile intent, the Chinese clearly fear that the Soviet forces could be used either to destroy China's emerging nuclear capabilities or to interfere in the succession in support of pro-Soviet elements. In response to the Soviet buildup and to initiatives taken by Washington, the Chinese began in 1971 to improve their relations with the United States. President Nixon's visit to China in 1972, Secretary of State Henry Kissinger's frequent trips to Peking, the exchange of liaison offices and the rapid expansion of cultural and economic relations have all symbolized the new Sino-American rapprochement.

Détente with the United States has provided a quick and inexpensive way of improving China's deterrence posture. Not only has it reduced the likelihood of a Sino-American war (a prospect that was not altogether remote during the escalation of the Vietnam conflict in 1965 and early 1966), but it has also raised doubts in Moscow about American reaction to a possible Sino-Soviet war. No longer can the Soviet Union assume that Washington would take a pro-Soviet, or even a neutral, position in the event of war between Russia and China.

Finally, while still not a major trading nation, China has begun to rely substantially on imports of agricultural products and advanced technology to meet some of its economic goals. The purchase of machinery and industrial plants from abroad has helped China develop its airline and its steel, petrochemical and fertilizer industries. Imports of grain and cotton, much of which came from the United States, helped tide China through its poor harvest in 1972.

Foreign Policy Under Attack

The success of China's foreign policy since the Cultural Revolution was perhaps demonstrated most dramatically by the Nixon and Tanaka visits to Peking in 1972, China's entry to the UN, and China's expanding diplomatic contacts and trade relations around the world. Despite these successes, however, much of Chou's foreign policy has become a controversial issue in Chinese domestic politics. Both during and after the Lin Piao affair, for instance, Chou was apparently criticized for his willingness to maintain friendly relations with nonprogressive third world governments and for his relatively cool attitude toward revolutionary movements in the third world.

Moreover, Chou's promotion of economic and cultural relations with the West has also been the target of criticism in recent months. Some more radical Chinese leaders seem to believe that the kind of advanced technology available from the West is unsuited to China's economy. If adopted, they fear, it would begin to promote the kind of differences between city and countryside, and between skilled and unskilled workers, that the Cultural Revolution was meant to eliminate. In addition, like many 19th-century Chinese intellectuals, some of today's leaders argue that the import of Western technology cannot be divorced from the import of Western ideas and values, particularly if economic relations are accompanied, as they have been recently, by cultural exchanges. They believe that China's efforts to create a new culture emphasizing equality, self-sacrifice and community would be seriously crippled by exposure to Western individualism and competitiveness. Finally, large-scale trade has the connotation of dependence on the outside world—an idea abhorrent to those who seek to demonstrate that China can develop as a strong, self-reliant member of the international community.

What of the policy of rapprochement with the United States? Here, too, there is evidence that Chou's policies have come under attack. Although the Chinese have gained some advantages from their new relationship with America, the radicals apparently have argued, the United States has gotten the better of the bargain. Sino-American détente facilitated American withdrawal from Indochina and may also have helped accelerate improvement in

Soviet-American relations: both substantial benefits for Washington. But on issues important to China, the radicals complain, little has been resolved. Fighting continues in Vietnam and Cambodia, only slight progress has been made in reconciling the differences between the two Koreas, the American commitment to Taiwan still seems strong and Washington shows few signs of moving rapidly toward the establishment of full diplomatic relations with Peking.

Because of these criticisms, foreign policy is an area in which Chou's political position is vulnerable. Any setbacks in the international arena could cost him support among both radicals and military leaders. As a result, just as Chou compromised with the radicals on certain domestic issues in 1973 and early 1974, so has he seemed to change his position on some foreign policy questions. In recent months, Chou has been voicing greater support for revolution in the third world. There have been small but unmistakeable signs of a cooling of Sino-American relations. As in domestic affairs, however, there have been areas in which Chou has been reluctant to compromise. Chinese officials have recently reiterated, for example, that China does not intend to change its policies of expanding trade with the United States and the West—at least, not under its present leadership.

Implications for American Policy

Because of the controversial nature of foreign policy in China, the future of Sino-American relations could be significantly influenced by the outcome of the succession. If the radicals come to power, there could be greater Chinese hostility toward the United States, a reduction in China's economic and cultural relations with the West, and increased support for national liberation movements in the third world. If the moderates continue in power, it is likely that China will remain willing to improve its relations with the United States, although it might also seek a limited détente with the Soviet Union.

The possibility that Sino-American relations might deteriorate as a result of the succession raises some crucial questions for American policy. Can the United States do anything to influence the succession in China, so as to ensure the victory of the moderates and improve the chances of continued détente? Here, the answer is almost certainly No. Some observers, noting that Chou has been criticized for his management of Sino-American relations, have proposed that the United States should immediately make a dramatic gesture toward Peking, such as an offer of full diplomatic recognition. Such a move, they have argued, would help vindicate Chou's foreign policy and strengthen him in his struggle with more radical leaders. But these proposals ignore the fact that the outcome of the succession will be determined primarily by economic and political conditions inside China, which the United States can not hope to influence. Moreover, any overt American attempt to influence the succession might well have an effect opposite to what was intended. It is best to recognize that the succession is a Chinese affair, in which the United States can only be a spectator, not a participant.

Even though the United States can not hope to influence the succession, however, it can actively encourage Mao's successors, whoever they may be, to continue the process of rapprochement. Unfortunately, recent developments in China, along with Washington's failure to make any substantial initiatives toward Peking since early 1973, have considerably slowed the improvement in relations between the two countries. If the United States can restore momentum to détente, it could increase the chances that the Sino-American rapprochement will survive the transition and continue under Mao's successors. As an immediate step to restore this kind of momentum, Washington should move more rapidly to solve two trade issues of particular concern to the Chinese: the granting of most-favored tariff treatment to China, and the releasing of Chinese assets in the United States frozen during the Korean war. Over a longer period, Washington should vigorously seek ways of completing the normalization of diplomatic relations with Peking and resolving the difficult and sensitive issue of Taiwan. In all these areas and in its cultural exchanges with China the United States should work to create relationships in which both sides enjoy equality and mutual benefit, as provided in the Shanghai communiqué of February 1972.

As we attempt to continue the process of rapprochement, however, Americans should also recognize the possibility of a temporary deterioration in Sino-American relations as China enters the post-Maoist era. As many historians have pointed out, Americans' attitudes toward China have tended to fluctuate rapidly and dramatically over the past 150 years. Improvements in our relations with China have created moods of optimism, goodwill and even euphoria: while periods of tension have led to disillusionment, hostility and a sense of betrayal. We must not again permit temporary setbacks to create lasting damage to our relations with the Chinese. It is imperative that Americans develop a more balanced, more knowledgeable, and therefore more stable understanding of China. Such understanding cannot guarantee, of course, that Sino-American relations will continue to improve. But without it, there can be little hope for a lasting détente.

Talking It Over

In this discussion guide you will find discussion questions and reading references. These are suggestions only—a starting point to help you plan a study-group program or a classroom teaching unit.

Discussion Questions

What, in your opinion, are some of the more important accomplishments of China? What are some of its failures?

What were the major issues involved in the rise and fall from power of Liu Shao-ch'i and Lin Piao?

What were the issues involved in the Cultural Revolution? Was it a success or a failure?

Controversy over the correct method of modernization has been a continuing feature of China's evolution. What is the significance of the controversy for Mao's succession? What are the broad issues involved? What are the specific issues as they affect: the roles of the party, bureaucracy and army, industrial and agricultural development, education?

The author outlines three possible scenarios for Mao's succession. Which, in your opinion, is the most likely to come to pass? Why? Which outcome, in your view, would be in the best interests of the United States? Why?

What are the foreign policy implications for China of the problem of Mao's succession?

What are the foreign policy implications for the United States of the succession problem? Do you think there is anything the United States can do or should do to affect the outcome?

READING REFERENCES

Barnett, A. Doak, *Uncertain Passage: China's Transition to the Post-Mao Era.* Washington, Brookings Institution, 1974. (Paperback.)

Baum, Richard, ed., *China in Ferment: Perspectives on the Cultural Revolution.* Englewood Cliffs, Prentice-Hall, 1971. (Paperback.)

Bianco, Lucien, *The Origins of the Chinese Revolution, 1915-1949.* Stanford, Stanford University Press, 1971. (Paperback.)

Bradsher, Henry S., "China: The Radical Offensive." *Asian Survey,* November 1973.

Bridgham, Philip, "The Fall of Lin Piao." *China Quarterly,* July-September 1973.

Donnithorne, Audrey, "China's Cellular Economy: Some Economic Trends Since the Cultural Revolution." *China Quarterly,* October/December 1972.

Fairbank, John K., *The United States and China,* 3rd rev.ed. Cambridge, Mass., Harvard University Press, 1971. (Paperback.)

Gardner, John, "Educated Youth and Urban-Rural Inequalities, 1958-66" in John W. Lewis, ed., *The City in Communist China,* Stanford, Stanford University Press, 1971.

Macciocchi, Maria, *Daily Life in Revolutionary China.* New York, Monthly Review Press, 1973. (Paperback.)

MacFarquhar, Roderick, "China After the 10th Congress." *World Today,* December 1973.

Oksenberg, Michel, "China: the Convulsive Society." *Headline Series* No. 203. New York, Foreign Policy Association, December 1970..

—————————————, ed., *China's Developmental Experience.* New York, Praeger for The Academy of Political Science, Columbia University, 1973. (Paperback.)

Rice, Edward E., *Mao's Way.* Berkeley, University of California Press, 1972. (Paperback.)

Schram, Stuart R., ed., *Authority, Participation and Cultural Change in China.* Cambridge, Mass., Cambridge University Press, 1973. (Paperback.)

Terrill, Ross, *Eight Hundred Million: The Real China.* New York, Delta, 1972. (Paperback.)

Townsend, James, *Politics in China: A Country Study.* Boston, Little, 1974. (Paperback.)

The People's Republic of China: An Economic Assessment. Joint Economic Committee, U.S. Congress, 92nd Cong., 2nd sess., Washington, D.C., USGPO, 1972.

Vogel, Ezra, *Canton Under Communism: Programs and Politics in a Provincial Capital, 1949-1968.* Cambridge, Mass., Harvard University Press, 1969.

Whyte, Martin K., "Bureaucracy and Modernization in China: The Maoist Critique." *American Sociological Review,* April 1973.

Statement of Ownership, Management and Circulation

(Act of August 12, 1970; Section 3685, Title 39, United States Code)

1. Title of publication: HEADLINE SERIES.

2. Date of filing: September 30, 1974

3. Frequency of issue: 5 times a year — Feb., Apr., June, Oct., Dec.

4. Location of known office of publication: 345 E. 46th St., New York, N.Y. 10017.

5. Location of the headquarters or general business offices of the publishers: same as above.

6. Names and addresses of publisher, editor, and managing editor: Publisher — Foreign Policy Association, Inc., 345 E. 46th St., New York, N.Y. 10017; Editor — Norman Jacobs, 345 E. 46th St., New York, N.Y. 10017; Managing Editor — None.

7. Owner: (If owned by a corporation, its name and address must be stated and also immediately thereunder the names and addresses of stockholders owning or holding 1 percent or more of total amount of stock. If not owned by a corporation, the names and addresses of the individual owners must be given. If owned by a partnership or other unincorporated firm, its name and address, as well as that of each individual must be given.) Foreign Policy Association, Inc., 345 E. 46th St., New York, N. Y. 10017; Samuel P. Hayes, President, 345 E. 46th St., New York, N. Y. 10017; Arthur B. Toan, Jr., Treasurer, c/o Price Waterhouse & Co., 1251 Ave. of the Americas, New York, N. Y. 10020.

8. Known bondholders, mortgagees, and other security holders owning or holding 1 percent or more of total amount of bonds, mortgages or other securities: (If there are none, so state) none.

9. Not applicable.

10. For Completion by Nonprofit Organizations Authorized to Mail at Special Rates (Section 132.122, Postal Manual): The purpose, function, and nonprofit status of this organization and the exempt status for Federal income tax purposes have not changed during preceding 12 months.

11. Extent and Nature of Circulation	Average No. Copies Each Issue During Preceding 12 Months	Actual Number of Copies of Single Issue Published Nearest to Filing Date
A. Total no. copies printed (Net Press Run)	15,771	14,800
B. Paid Circulation 1. Sales through dealers and carriers, street vendors and counter sales	4,926	419
2. Mail subscriptions.	8,103	8,429
C. Total paid circulation	13,029	8,884
D. Free distribution by mail, carrier or other means 1. Samples, complimentary, and other free copies	265	237
2. Copies distributed to news agents, but not sold	None	None
E. Total distribution (Sum of C and D)	13,294	9,085
F. Office use, left-over, unaccounted, spoiled after printing	2,477	5,715
G. Total (Sum of E & F—should equal net press run shown in A)	15,771	14,800

I certify that the statements made by me above are correct and complete.

DON DENNIS,
Business Manager